# how to get really rich

# BRIAN ROSNER

how to get
really
rich

## A sharp look at
## the religion of greed

with poems by Richard Firmin

Inter-Varsity Press

INTER-VARSITY PRESS
38 De Montfort Street, Leicester LE1 7GP, England

*First published 1999*

**British Library Cataloguing in Publication Data**
A catalogue record for this book is available from the British Library.

ISBN 0–85111–649–3

Set in Garamond
Typeset in Great Britain
Printed in Great Britain by
Caledonian International Book Manufacturing Ltd

# CONTENTS

To Elizabeth, Emily and William

# Foreword

There are many signs in our society that greed has got out of hand. Incomes are double today what they were a generation ago, and technology has eased the burden of many routine tasks. So why do we need to work even harder, and for even longer hours? Is it really out of economic necessity, or simply to afford more toys for the children?

Why is there still such competition between political parties to reduce taxes, even when this leads to industry-crippling interest rates and loss of jobs? The result is that the rich just get richer and the poor poorer. And where will the government find the money to pay for essential improvements in education and health-care provision?

The Bible tells us to look after the poor, especially the 'fatherless and widows'. Our cities are now full of fatherless teenagers and abandoned wives. And we, in our greed, have abandoned them too.

Then there's the time-bomb of pensions. A generation which puts off having children because they spoil its enjoyment of the good things of life is going against the wisdom of the ages. We need children to look after us when we can no longer look after ourselves. The falling birth rate has created a huge gap in the income needed to provide the pensions of this high-spending generation.

No government, of any political persuasion, can afford to ignore the opinion of voters. If Brian Rosner's well-reasoned appeal to the conscience can influence individuals, it may succeed in making an impact on government policies which promote greed.

The sin of covetousness, laid bare by this excellent book, shows that Christians must be part of the counter-culture, resistant to the TV ads and to the skewed priorities of our consumer culture. Giving is the antidote to selfishness, but is also a command for Christians. If we take that command seriously, maybe the world will take us seriously.

*Sir Fred Catherwood*

# Preface

This book consists of Christian reflections on greed, contentment and giving in the modern world. Needless to say, the chosen title, *How to Get Really Rich*, was thought preferable to this rather dull, if accurate, description of the book's contents. It is not a balanced and irenic survey of the Bible's teaching on possessions.[1] Nor is it a book of practical advice on how we should deal with our money. It would be less than honest, however, to say that I am not interested in changing behaviour, both mine and yours. The book is an attempt to disturb our pockets, not with practical tips and specific appeals, but rather by warming our hearts and clearing our heads. I am convinced that such change best comes about by changing the way we think about ourselves, the world and God. This is the strategy Paul

11

recommends in Romans 12:2: 'Be transformed by the renewing of your mind.'

Our look at greed is 'sharp' in the sense of forceful and satirical, in that when reflecting on the teaching relevant to our topic in the Bible, the dominant notes struck are those of irony and ridicule. Money is one of those areas where the Bible stands against us and offers us an alternative vision. The satire, however, stops short of outright scorn, since I make no claim to being anything but complicit in the follies the book attempts to expose. On the contrary, if the book affords any insight, it is usually due to first-hand experience of the sins it condemns. Whether the book is sharp in the sense of incisive is for the reader to decide.

Following the Bible's lead, greed is analysed as a *religion*, as nothing less than a sophisticated form of idolatry. The book sets out to deliver both a challenge and comfort to people who feel dissatisfied with the materialism of our age.

In 1996–7 I spent a sabbatical at the University of Tübingen in Germany as a Humboldt Fellow doing research for an academic monograph on the subject of greed and idolatry in the ancient world. The obvious relevance of this material to the modern world slowly dawned on me, at which point the idea for this book was conceived. A number of people have helped in various ways with its delivery. Thanks are due to Anke and Matthias Kumpf, Sheana and Peter Brown, Tracy and Graham Robertson, Kevin Reid, Alan Storkey, Audrey Dawson, my parents and parents-in-law, my wife Leanne, and IVP editor Stephanie Heald. I am particularly grateful to Richard Firmin, not only for writing the poems (pp. 30, 45, 47, 61, 71, 93 and 102) and acrostic (p. 149), but for giving me the final push to finish. The book is dedicated to three of my treasures, the priceless Elizabeth and Emily and that wee gem William.

Greed … is idolatry.

Colossians 3:5

Godliness with contentment is great gain.

1 Timothy 6:6

# 1
# UNMASKING GREED

Nothing beats the exhilaration of trading on the floor at a major stock exchange, so I'm told. All of us have seen pictures of the frenzied buying and selling in which a fortune can be won or lost depending on whether the deal is made at precisely the right moment. Three of the slogans on Wall Street sum up the sentiments of most of those involved: 'Buy or die' and 'Lunch is for wimps' proclaim the urgency of the activity; and 'Greed is good' captures its driving motivation.

Most of us would stop short of affirming that greed is good. That is to state the matter rather too strongly. We have a more nuanced attitude towards money. If asked what is more important to us, we would not hesitate to put family and friends ahead of material things. We are also quite prepared to condemn the massive pay rises which company directors grant themselves as nothing less than obscene. And we shake our heads in disgust at the wanton acquisitiveness of an Imelda Marcos, whose collection of shoes outnumbered most people's stamp collections, or at the self-destructive avarice of a Nick Leeson, whose lust for money brought down Barings Bank.

Yet our attitude to money can be quite contradictory. Although, when speaking generally about the human condition, we say that everyone loves money, we are usually not willing to say the same in reference to ourselves.

Money is in fact the last great social taboo. Whereas once it was thought rude or at least tactless to speak about sex or politics in polite conversation, these days it seems that only the subject of money is unmentionable. In most western societies at least, one is not permitted to ask individuals how much they earn or what they do with their money. When it comes to money, most of us are very secretive.

Why is this the case? The psychologist Dorothy Rowe puts it down to shame, humiliation and envy.[1] Money is a measure of success. There is shame in being hard up and pride in being well-heeled. An amusing example concerns the unfavourable publicity the British Chancellor of the Exchequer received when it was disclosed that the limit on his credit card was surprisingly low. For many people, to know someone else's net worth would evoke one of two responses: either envy or disdain. Money is the simplest measure of whether you are winning at the game of life.

Most people, it is true, would not say that greed is good. If the phenomenon of national lotteries is anything to go by, however, the vast majority of us are rather keen on the idea of getting really rich. Christians are, it seems, no different. A survey of regular churchgoers in the USA found that almost 90% say greed is a sin; fewer than 20% say they were ever taught that wanting a lot of money is wrong, and almost 80% say that they wish they had more money than they do.[2]

Insatiability is of course not unique to modern western civilization. Greed has always been with us. As Miroslav Volf has observed, however, 'cultural acceptance, even encouragement, of insatiability is unique to modernity ... The inactive virus of insatiability broke out with capitalism in a general epidemic.'[3] It is probably fair to say that even though greed remains a vice in most people's minds, it has been devalued.

One preacher suggested four reasons why Christians do not often hold greed to be as grave as, for instance, sexual immorality: 'Because, (1) it is so common; (2) because it is found among those who make pretensions to refinement and even religion; (3) because it is not so easy to define what is covetousness, as it is to define impurity of life; and (4) because the public conscience is seared, and the mind blinded to the low and grovelling character of the sin.'[4]

Greed today is, by comparison with times past, a

trivial sin. 'Don't be greedy' is most commonly heard when someone wants a second piece of chocolate cake. Greed may even be said to be a public good, the engine which drives economic progress. The condemnation of greed is the last thing in the mind of the media when interviewing or reporting a story about some fabulously wealthy celebrity. And even though, if you stop to think about it, greed makes many people's lives a misery, modern psychology generally does not take greed to be a problem worth treating. Try asking the relatives of a workaholic or a compulsive gambler if they agree. A retired priest recounted that in his long years of service all kinds of sins and concerns were confessed to him in the confessional, but never once the sin of greed.

In politics, and even in music and sport, 'the bottom line' is apparently all that counts these days. Political campaigns are regularly fought by appealing without shame or qualms to the greed of voters. Which party is promising the biggest tax cut? Other values are swept aside compared to the party's ability to manage the economy to the end of enriching its citizens. Ex-Beatle George Harrison recently lamented the modern recording industry's raw commercialism: 'Whatever you play, the most important thing is to sell and make money. It's got nothing to do with talent.'[5] Vexatious litigation is frequently what follows success; as one manager put it: 'Where there's a hit, there's a writ.' One football fan made a similar observation about a report concerning his team, Manchester United plc, which dwelt on a £44 million turnover and an £11 million profit, and mentioned only in passing their winning the Premier League and the FA Cup: 'Manchester United, with its great history and inspiring legends, has grown cynical and arrogant in its mad pursuit of money ... Bigger salaries have made players and managers just as greedy as the clubs.'[6]

Greed is almost an Olympic sport, if the behaviour of certain members of the International Olympic Committee is anything to go by. A select band of its members apparently received money, free medical care and educational scholarships in exchange for their votes concerning the destination of the 2002 Olympic flame. The traditional slogan, 'Faster, higher, stronger', has been adapted, as one newspaper editorial put it, to 'Cash, cheques, credit cards'. Those who offered the 'incentives' to the IOC members saw no cause for blushing, claiming in their defence that they had simply been following a long-established (if not terribly honourable) Olympic tradition.

How many tales of woe could be told which involve the destruction of families over the matter of the Will? As someone once said, where there is a Will, there is a war. Many a wealthy family has been torn apart over the inheritance that a child had expected and didn't get. Apparently, the bigger the cake, the more we fight over our share. That money is a cause of domestic strife in families which are not well off also goes without saying. In such cases the lack of money can of course be a genuine factor, but more often than not one party will be quick to accuse the other of acting out of greed.

Greed is often the motivation behind a whole range of other more obviously destructive behaviours. In the USA there was a rise in professional murders from fewer than 1,000 in 1980 to over 5,000 in 1997. The FBI puts this down to tougher divorce laws, which force the guilty party to fork out more money. Apparently, if the figures add up, aggrieved spouses hire assassins to kill their partners. One agent, who regularly poses as a hit-man in order to apprehend the culprits, explains their motives: 'They're basically driven by greed and jealousy. The clients are treating somebody's life as just an annoying obstacle to what they want ... People think: they want my money. They deserve to die.'[7]

It is difficult to comprehend the fact that the greed of one person can have an adverse effect on the lives of tens of millions of people. Nevertheless it is true. Indonesia's economic problems in the late 1990s, which led to widespread poverty and the eruption of numerous riots, doubtless have complex causes; the blame cannot be easily apportioned. The fact that President Suharto's personal wealth has been estimated at $16 billion and that of his family at $40 billion, however, cannot be overlooked. It is a cruel coincidence that the International Monetary Fund's rescue plan for the country's ailing economy came to about the same figure.[8] The long-running joke in Indonesia is that so pervasive is the Suharto family's reach into the economy that they start profiting from your visit as soon as you arrive at the airport in Jakarta: if you buy a packet of cigarettes, take a taxi, pay the toll on the road into the city, check into a hotel, and so on, with each step money goes into the family's pockets.

Greedy behaviour is taken for granted, as can be seen from the way we respond to the exceptions. Aaron Feuerstein owned a textile mill in Massachusetts. Two weeks before Christmas the plant was burned to the ground. Everyone assumed that he would take the insurance money and run, to the financial detriment of the employees. After all, what else would a businessman with any sense do? Instead, Feuerstein told his staff that they would be kept on full pay over the holiday period and given a Christmas bonus. In other words, he did the decent thing. Apparently, decency is abnormal. President Clinton invited Mr Feuerstein to his State of the Union address and there proclaimed him an American hero.[9]

It would in fact be hard to understand the modern world without some reference to greed. The second half of the twentieth century was dominated by the Cold War and the rise and fall of communism. It is pure irony that the system which set itself against the greed of capitalism was eventually brought down in part by the greed of its own governing classes.

You could say that there are three major current threats to our existence as individuals and societies: pollution, terrorism and crime. In each case greed can take a good share of the credit. Pollution is caused and continues to be caused by human unwillingness to pay the price for the cleaner alternatives. We don't lack the technology, just the will. On any reckoning, climatic change due to the effects of pollution could cause major 'natural' disasters in the days to come. In most cases of terrorism, each side accuses the other of some form of greed, whether involving people, land or property. Greed also fits both sides of the equation in many cases of crime. Thieves steal because they want more and often because they perceive the victims as having more than their fair share.

## Christian attitudes to greed

Christians have not always regarded greed so lightly. In fact, according to the New Testament, greed qualifies as one of the most serious of sins. The earliest Christians were told not just to avoid greed, but to watch out for it (Luke 12:15), to flee from it (1 Tim. 6:11) or to kill it (Col. 3:5). Greed is described in most unflattering terms. It is 'a root of all kinds of evil' (1 Tim. 6:10), one of the twelve things which come out of individuals and defile them (Mark 7:20–22), evidence of a darkened understanding or a depraved mind (Eph. 4:18–19; Rom. 1:28–29). Worst of all, greed is said to be a form of idolatry (see chapter 2). Jesus went as far as to tell a parable which is directed specifically against greed, in which God chastises the protagonist with the words, 'You fool!' (Luke 12:16–20). Furthermore, greed is thought to lead to other sins, including theft, pride and sexual immorality.

Indeed, there is a wealth of evidence from the Old Testament and early Jewish moral teaching which supports a link between greed and injustice. Most of the hostility to wealth which can be found in the Old Testament is linked to the failure of the rich to act justly towards the stranger, the widow, the orphan and the poor. The wealthy man is equated with the wicked (Ps. 10:3), the violent (Prov. 11:6) and the proud (Prov. 15:25; 16:19; Is. 2:7, 11; 13:11, 17; Jer. 51:13). The rich are those who 'carry out wicked schemes' (Ps. 37:7) and offer bribes (Prov. 17:18). Furthermore, wealth is often linked with wickedness (Prov. 10:12; 11:28; 22:1; cf. Ps. 37:16; Prov. 15:16; 16:8; 17:1; 28:6). The first ethical concern to be mentioned in Proverbs is the band of outlaws whose goal it is to 'get all sorts of valuable things' and to 'fill [their] houses with plunder' (1:13); wisdom warns that such people 'rush into sin' and are 'swift to shed blood' (1:16). In Proverbs 19:22 it is taken for granted that the greedy are liars. In Micah 2:2, 'They covet fields and seize them'.

Similarly, Philo observes that 'injustice is bred by anxious thought for the means of life and for money-making'.[10] Riches and injustice are associated in one of the Dead Sea Scrolls: 'men of injustice ... who are zealous after wealth'.[11] And an early Jewish rabbinic commentary states that 'if you desire you will covet; and if you covet you will tyrannize and rob'.[12]

In Revelation 18, where the fall of Babylon is announced, her sumptuous wealth and extravagance are tainted when the merchants' list of cargo, which opens with 'gold, silver, jewels and pearls,' closes emphatically with 'slaves, that is, human souls' (verses 12–13, Revised Standard Version), suggesting that the city's prosperity and luxury rely on brutality and contempt for human life. This impression is confirmed in 18:21, where Babylon is condemned as a blood-shedding city of violence, produced and maintained by military force. Babylon epitomizes the ruthlessness of greed.

If you were to ask the apostle Paul or someone else in the early church to construct a profile of your average pagan, someone who does not know the true and living God, you would probably have got a three-point sermon in response. Early Jews and Christians alike condemned the Gentiles first of all for their idolatry, then for their sexual immorality and finally for their greed. In Luke 12:22–30, for example, the Gentiles are described as those whose lifestyle is characterized by a relentless seeking after material things. In the letter of Polycarp, written soon after the close of the New Testament, greed is specifically distinguished as being a mark of the heathen (11:2).

On only two occasions in Acts is the opposition to the early church specifically non-Jewish. In both cases financial considerations caused the problems. When Paul in Philippi cast the demon of divination out of the slave girl (16:16–18), her owners, who were incensed over their loss of income (verse 19), brought him before the magistrates to be flogged and imprisoned (verses 20–24). Later, Paul's stand against idolatry led to a riot instigated by the silversmiths who made the shrines to the goddess Artemis and regarded the apostle as a threat to their livelihood (19:23–41).

To put the matter the other way around, greed not only suits a pagan's lifestyle, it is also not a fitting behaviour for someone who knows God. In Colossians 3 Paul encourages the church not to be greedy because such behaviour is incompatible with a genuinely Christian lifestyle. Likewise, according to 1 Corinthians 5:11, people who claim to be Christians and are nevertheless greedy do not belong in the church and should be excluded.

Christendom before the modern period took greed just as seriously. In the fourth century, Zeno of Verona declared simply: 'God is right to hate greed.'[13] The greedy are as insatiable as hell, according to Basil the Great: 'Hell never says enough is enough; neither does greed ever say enough.'[14] Ambrose thought greed so central that he spoke of the primal sin, that of Adam in the garden, not as original sin, but as 'original greed'.

In the Middle Ages an important vehicle for moral teaching was the list of so-called seven deadly sins: pride, lust, gluttony, sloth, anger, envy and greed. Although Gregory the Great placed pride ahead of greed at the top of the list, in the numerous expositions in the centuries following him greed usually took pride of place. Medical metaphors were often used to describe the effects greed can have on people. Greed was not only a deadly sin but a deadly disease. Greed was commonly thought to be the spiritual equivalent of dropsy, which involves an insatiable thirst for water even though the body is already filled with fluid. The more the afflicted person tries to satisfy the thirst, the more it is

# The six deadly sins

He entered the confessional –
This sinner's cup was brimming full.
    He'd counted them – the score was six;
T'was time to shed this loathsome mix.

'O Father, I have slept around
With many women in this town.
    It seems my Lust just knows no bounds,
Though with my wife no fault is found.

And Father, Envy racks my mind –
My neighbour bugs me double time;
    He's four cars now, I've only three –
He *has* to keep ahead of me.

He asked me round to see the Merc;
I can't believe the stupid berk:
    My Anger got the best of me –
I told him where to stick the key.

I s'pose he'd touched my wounded Pride –
I said, 'You'll get no better ride
    Than in my Jag, which, by the way,
Is British, mate, the best, OK?'

I left him then; he'd worn me through
And partly spoiled my midday snooze.
    My wife awoke me with an oath,
Complaining I'd succumbed to Sloth.

But Father, take a look at me,
My favourite sin is Gluttony.
    I eat four solid meals a day
And in between just snack away.

But now I've told you all of them –
Forgive me, Father, grant pardon.'

'O son, I might, if that were all,
But six is *not*, you may recall,
    The total of the deadly sins –
The Seventh's where your road begins.'

stimulated. So it was thought to be the case with greed.[15]

In the Protestant Reformation greed maintained its bad reputation. According to Martin Luther, for instance, greed causes unbelief, and unbelief causes greed. Luther took the fourth request of the Lord's prayer, 'Give us today our daily bread', as a call to shun greed. He also urged every Christian to undertake regular and earnest prayer against this dangerous vice.

## This book

Greed has been glamorized and is a forgotten sin. A major goal of this book is to reveal its true hideousness and to restore its hard-won, well-deserved reputation. Although greed can be profitably analysed in terms of sociological, psychological and economic factors, its root cause can be understood only with the help of theology. Greed is a theological problem. To leave the question of God out of our attempts to understand greed is to treat the problem superficially. Whether or not the reader is a Christian, my goal is to show that God offers in his Word, the Bible, not only a penetrating diagnosis of greed, but also and more importantly the ultimate cure for greed.

This book is in effect an exposition of two short biblical texts. Chapters 2–5 ponder Colossians 3:5, 'Greed … is idolatry'. Chapters 6–8 spell out the implications of 1 Timothy 6:6, 'Godliness with contentment is great gain'.

Writing a book against greed could be said to be doomed to failure from the start. 'Deploring money and its effects is a treasured occupation for those people who like to feel virtuous,' writes Dorothy Rowe. 'Doing so is as useful as deploring the fact that we need air to breathe.'[16] Indeed, many have observed that greed (of one sort or another) is inevitable for the human species. Rowe puts the matter simply: 'I think that the only way to give up being greedy is to die.'[17] The philosopher Immanuel Kant likewise observed that 'insatiability belongs to the basic makeup of human beings'.[18] And the theologian Eberhard Jüngel concurs: 'Striving for more is human.'[19]

Thus in one sense the only hope in the fight against greed is not to fight those insatiable urges for more, but to redirect them. This, as we shall see, is what the Bible recommends. There is nothing wrong with wanting to get really rich, as long as riches are properly defined.

# 2
# SECRET IDOLATRY

There is no more serious charge in the Bible than that of idolatry. Idolatry called for the strictest punishment, elicited the most disdainful polemic and prompted the most extreme measures of avoidance. The theological grounds for the judgment of idolatry is the jealousy of God, which inevitably leads him to stern action: 'Do not follow other gods ... for the LORD your God ... is a jealous God and his anger will burn against you, and he will destroy you from the face of the land' (Deut. 6:14–15; cf. Josh. 24:19–20; Ps. 78:58–64; Zeph. 1:18).

The crime of idolatry is mentioned in the Mishnah (the second-century AD rabbinical collection of the oral law) only to clarify the question of culpability and punishment.[1] The majority opinion accorded idolatry the punishment of stoning, the severest punishment of all, and it was ranked first of the three commandments which should never be transgressed by a Jew (the other two being against illicit sex and bloodshed). That idolatry was not only threatened with severe punishment but also received it can be illustrated on a national level. One of the lowest points in Israel's history was the destruction of Solomon's temple, which Rabbi Yohanon ben Torta blamed on idolatry, illicit sexual relations and bloodshed.

In the Old Testament, disgust and contempt for idolatry are communicated by several derogatory terms used to describe the idols. Idols are 'unclean things', 'weak' or 'worthless things', 'that which is insubstantial', and a 'vanity' or 'emptiness'. The Israelites were not simply to avoid idolatry; the language of prohibition could hardly be more emotive and urgent; they are 'utterly [to] abhor and detest' the heathen gods (Deut. 7:25–26). For both Jews and Christians in the ancient world, the charge of idolatry evoked horror and alarm. The Church Father Tertullian (c. AD 200) did not exaggerate when he described idolatry as the 'principal crime of the human race, the highest guilt charged upon the world, [and] the whole procuring cause of judgment'.[2]

## The equation of greed with idolatry

For this reason it is surprising to learn that the New Testament equates greed with idolatry on no fewer than four occasions. Colossians 3:5 states that 'greed

… is idolatry', and Ephesians 5:5 that the 'greedy person … is an idolater'. And according to Matthew 6:24 and Luke 16:13, Jesus portrayed wealth and possessions as a master that rivals God: 'No-one can serve two masters. Either he will hate the one and love the other, or he will be devoted to one and despise the other. You cannot serve both God and Money [literally, Mammon].'

A possible fifth condemnation of greed in terms of idolatry appears in Revelation. In Revelation's announcement of the fall of Babylon, the economic and religious dimensions of her sins are not easily separated. The economic greed of Rome, to which the symbol of Babylon in the original setting of the book refers, has a peculiarly religious guise. The harlot's cloth in 18:16–17 not only underlines Rome's extravagant luxury but also alludes ironically to the sacred garments of the priests in Exodus 28:5, 15–17. Likewise, the reference to Babylon deceiving the nations in 18:23 is evocative of the effect of idols on their worshippers. Finally, the counterpoint to Babylon's wealth is the spiritual wealth of the new Jerusalem in the following chapters, suggesting that there is more to the greed of Rome than meets the eye. It may be that Revelation 18, with its use of fornication language, condemns the influence of Roman imperial religion, alongside a forthright con-demnation of Rome's economic exploitation of the Empire. Alternatively, the two emphases may be seen as inextricably bound together, with Rome's eco-nomic sins being portrayed in religious terms. Rome / Babylon may well represent the very embodiment of idolatrous greed.[3]

Is greed then idolatry? Can it really be that bad? Does the love of money really pose such a serious threat to God? What are we to make of these verses? Surely they are simply ill-considered exaggerations, or at best religious rhetoric designed to arrest our attention but not to engage our minds?

## Is greed idolatry?

Greed and idolatry in the ancient world in fact had a lot in common. First, both focused attention on items made of gold and silver. In biblical and Jewish tradition these two metals are frequently associated with both the greedy, who can be called literally 'lovers of silver', and the idols of pagan worship, beginning with the golden calf. Secondly, both the greedy and the idolater visited pagan temples, the latter for obvious reasons, and the former since in antiquity the temples operated not only as places of worship but as banks. And thirdly, both greed and idolatry, according to moral exhortation found in the New Testament, were considered to be of such gravity that they ought to be 'fled'; greed in 1 Timothy 6:11 and idolatry in 1 Corinthians 10:14.

In our day, whatever we make of the words of Jesus and Paul, it is worth noting that people with no religious commitment have observed the almost religious function money performs for many people. *The Oxford English Dictionary*, for instance, defines materialism in religious terms, as 'devotion to material needs or desires, to the neglect of spiritual matters'. Two articles in *The Times* went even further. Alexander Frean wrote on 5 September 1997: 'Bereft of employment security and increasingly detached from traditional faith in religion, people appear to have elevated material objects … virtually to objects of faith' (p. 11). Dorothy Rowe suggested on 1 September 1997 that such devotion to material things is bound to fail: 'Even if we achieve what the world is pleased to acknowledge as success, we discover that the seizing of it fails to satisfy the hunger of our spiritual expectation' (p. 34).

As it turns out, the judgment that greed is idolatry is both an incisive social critique of modern society and a profound insight into Christian theology and ethics.

If the greedy are guilty of worshipping their money and possessions, what then is religion? There are many different answers to this question. Some define religion in psychological terms, stressing the notion of the holy or the sacred, and people's response to it. Others look at the functions of religion, such as the quest to make sense of the ultimate problems of life and the attempt to integrate people into social units or communities of faith. Still others take a more popular approach, noticing elements common to all religions, including belief systems, rituals, symbols and ceremonies. No matter how it is defined, a good case can be made for concluding that greed qualifies as a religion.

There has never been a time in the history of the world when Jesus' and Paul's condemnations of greed as idolatry seemed more apt and made more sense than now. If people in the ancient world worshipped stocks and stones (Jer. 2:27; Hos. 4:12, Authorized Version), today is everywhere to be found the worship of stocks and shares. Sociologist John Boli is not exaggerating when he warns: 'We must come to terms with the depth of the problem [of materialism]: We are dealing with a highly institutionalised economic religion that must be confronted on its own terms, and many of the cultural underpinnings of that religion are, I believe, truly sacred to us all.'[4]

In western society in general the economy has achieved what can only be described as a status equal to that of the sacred. Like God, the economy, it is thought, is capable of supplying people's needs without limit. Also like God, the economy is mysterious, unknowable and intransigent. It has both great power and, despite the best managerial efforts of its associated clergy, great danger. It is an inexhaustible well of good(s) and is credited with prolonging life, giving health and enriching our lives. Money, in which we put our faith, and advertising, which we adore, are among its rituals. The economy also has its sacred symbols, which evoke undying loyalty, including company logos, product names and credit cards.

People today conduct their lives primarily in terms of economic religiosity. The economy is the ultimate source of value and, as a religion, confers value on those who participate in it. Not to participate in the economy is to lack any social worth, as many of those without paid employment have come to learn.

As a religion, the economy supplies solutions to the basic puzzles of life and help in negotiating them. The meaning of a person's life is found in full participation in the economy, as both a producer and a consumer. The purpose of life involves the full development of the individual's economic potential and the pursuit of material progress for the good of all. Scores of books and courses are available at every level to assist the faithful to realize their potential. Whereas once the most vivid and intense experiences of life were to be found in traditional religion, today they involve money rituals, whether at work, on holidays or shopping. The religion of money even has its creeds and dogmas, such as 'Money makes the world go round'.

The modern-day equivalent of the city cathedral is the major shopping mall. The centre of the community in every sense, such complexes are admired for their huge, costly edifices and their awe-inspiring architecture, which often includes an aesthetically pleasing internal space made of glass and stone. They are visited by 'pilgrims' from across the country and sometimes even from overseas. Visitors spend hours in such places (not to mention loads of money), drinking in the experience of being overwhelmed by the variety and beauty of the goods on offer before returning to their local shopping centres and their everyday lives the better for it.

The fact that money has taken on religious significance for many people is clear from the British National Lottery. The twice-weekly draw is televised and watched by millions of people. It bears a remarkable resemblance to a church service. There is a leader of worship, musical items, personal testimonies (to the life-transforming power of money) and the holy sacrament of releasing the balls. One popular presenter was even known to offer a prayer: 'I know I'm a sinner, but make me a winner!'

Traditional religions saw the home as the place where instruction could be carried out most effectively. The religion of money is no different, with both television and computers inculcating the good news for every age group. The average American watches about eighty-five television advertisements each and every day, all of which relentlessly and unequivocally advocate an ideology of consumption and materialism.

The once noble occupation of the evangelist spreading the gospel has also been replaced by a secular alternative. Someone distributing religious tracts outside a shopping centre is today regarded with suspicion and looked upon with scorn. Yet we take for granted the legitimacy of the person making an appeal on behalf of this or that product.

Some denominations of the Mammon religion in America even had a wicked power to struggle against, namely communism, or the 'evil empire' as President Reagan used to call it. The demise of communism has cemented the associations of goodness and piety which such circles attached to capitalism and materialism. Dorothy Rowe rather cynically contends that all Americans believe in three things: God, America and the Market. Perhaps there is a sense in which the boundaries between these three

# The punter's prayer

Give me some more cards to scratch,
Help me make the numbers match.
Tell me if this horse can run;
Be there when the wheel is spun.
I'm down on my knees but I plan to get bigger;
I know I'm a sinner, but make me a winner.

Give me some more cash to spend,
Clothe me in the latest trend.
Guide me on my shopping sprees;
Help me squeeze these jeans on, please!
I'm down on my knees and I dare not get
   bigger;
I know I'm a sinner, but let me grow thinner.

Tesco, Safeway, Sainsbury's,
I use them all, my loyalty's
To number one – food is food –
Fill my trolley if you would.
I'm down on my knees and the queue's getting
   bigger;
I know I'm a sinner, but fix me some dinner.

Can this lotion smooth my skin?
   Will aerobics keep me trim?
   Do I earn enough to spare?
   Should I buy the best healthcare?
I'm down on my knees and the light's growing
   dimmer;
I know I'm a sinner, but spare me the zimmer.

entities have become blurred.[5]

Traditional religion does not stand a chance against this new religion. It has been pushed to the sidelines. Boli explains: 'Religion may help us save our souls or understand the agony of life and death, but it cannot help us to obtain the vast array of goodnesses, meanings and purposes that are preferred in the economic realm.'[6] Alan Storkey sounds a similar note of despair: 'Christianity, despite all the warnings in the Gospels, has not even seen the challenge, the temptation, the lies, the enemy. We must consider sometime how completely the Christian community is unable to discern what is seeking to be the god of this age.'[7]

Some forms of Christianity have followed a time-honoured course in response to this newly ascendant religion: namely, syncretism, an attempt to cash in on the attraction of its beliefs and practices. The gospel of health, wealth and prosperity is the response of those who consider resistance to be of no avail. 'If you can't beat 'em, join 'em.' When such preachers proclaim that it is God's will for you to be healthy and wealthy, and that not to be so is evidence of your lack of faith, they fail to reveal only one thing: which god they are talking about.

Conversely, the much lamented but seldom resisted commercialization of the traditional religious festivals, such as Christmas, is a clear example of the takeover strategy of the religion of greed.

# We three kings

We three kings of industry are –
We sell videos, tellies and cars,
Microwaves, mowers, strimmers and
   blowers,
Mountain bikes, bass guitars ... and
      All that's shiny, all that's loud,
      All that makes you feel so proud;
      Makes you feel like some big wheel,
      While you just roll with the crowd.

We build kitchens, bathrooms and pools,
Triple-glazed windows, three-legged stools,
Four-poster beds; bespoke garden sheds
For storing collections of tools ... and
      All that's tasteless, all that's crass,
      All that's empty, weightless, gas,
      Fills the space within our race,
      Conforms and shapes the mindless
         mass.

We invent your every need,
We create desire to feed:
Fantasy fountains, mercury mountains,
Gifts to the goddess of greed ... and
      All that glitters, all that's brash,
      All that's bound to grab your cash;
      Keeps you yearning, never learning:
      Dust to dust and ash to ash.

The most disturbing thing about the fact that greed is idolatry is that hardly anybody owns up to being a worshipper. Imagine the response of disbelief in the local church if it were revealed that the vast majority of its members were secretly worshipping other gods. Yet if our analysis of the religion of money is right, the unthinkable may not be so far from the truth.

The most convincing evidence that greed is idolatry concerns the answer to a simple question: what do idolaters do with their idols which believers are meant to do with God? The answer is that they offer their idols love, trust and obedience. In each case, that is exactly what the greedy do with their money. There are various ways to define greed. Greed is wanting more money and possessions. Greed is the opposite of contentment. Greed is a refusal to share your possessions. And so on. Our approach in the following three chapters is to consider greed in terms of its driving motivations. What causes people to be insatiable and mean with respect to material things? Greed is driven by inordinate love, misplaced trust and forbidden service; as such greed is rightly condemned as idolatry.

# 3
# INORDINATE LOVE

*The New Shorter Oxford English Dictionary* defines the verb 'to worship' as: 'Honour or adore as divine or sacred, esp. with religious rites or ceremonies.'[1] By this definition, the greedy clearly do not worship their possessions. *The Oxford English Dictionary's* 'transferred' (or figurative) sense for 'worship' is probably more helpful for our purposes: worship is to 'regard with extreme respect, devotion, or love'.[2] If to worship something means to have great love for it, then the excessive love of money, for which the greedy are known, constitutes idolatrous worship.

This is certainly the way the majority of biblical commentators have understood the words 'Greed … is idolatry' in Colossians 3:5 (cf. Eph. 5:5). The Church Father Radalphus, for example, said: 'God, for each one of us, is what we honour above all else,

51

what we *admire and love* above all.'[3] The Reformer John Calvin agreed: '[The greedy person] sets all his *heart* and mind on them [material things], and forgets God ... You see then that the covetous abuse their riches by setting *their whole heart* upon them.'[4] And the biblical scholar J. B. Lightfoot adds: 'The covetous man sets up another object of worship besides God. There is a sort of religious purpose, a *devotion* of the soul, to greed, which makes the sin of the miser so hateful.'[5]

## The love of money

Love may be a many-splendoured thing, the subject of countless songs and works of fiction, but it is pretty difficult to define. There is a world of difference between the romantic love of a couple, the fraternal love experienced in a football team and the compassionate love of the nurse or aid worker, let alone between divine love, parental love, patriotic love and so on. Love can arise out of all sorts of motives and emotions, including physical attraction, affection, pity, wonder, gratitude and pride. You can love your spouse, your mates, the down-and-out, God, your parents and your country, not to mention your dog, your car, tomato ketchup and French mustard. Why and in what sense do the greedy love money?

In one sense the answer to this question is obvious enough. From the frenzied response to the glamorous prizes offered on the game shows which appear regularly on our televisions we may observe that if money can't buy love, most of us seem to think that it can buy happiness. Visible delight and palpable glee burst from the screens into our living-rooms as shining goods are dangled tantalizingly before perspiring contestants. Sneering aside, there is no doubt that money can bring great pleasure and comfort. Only a desert monk would pretend otherwise.

*Keep the Aspidistra Flying* was George Orwell's cynical advice on such matters, offered in his 1936 novel by the same name. The main character, Gordon Comstock, an idealistic young man, gives up the material comforts afforded by his job in an advertising agency to work as a part-time bookshop assistant in order to pursue his passion for writing. Falling in love with Rosemary, Gordon blames his new-found poverty for his failure in matters amorous. He gives up poetry and returns to his former job, setting to work on their campaign to market a product which masks foot odour (PP, 'pedic perspiration', a slogan inspired by the analogous BO, body odour). Comstock embraces again the middle-class values of owning furniture and paying bills. These are quizzically symbolized in the potted aspidistra, an ugly house plant with broad tapering leaves. This plant, which he dubs 'the tree of life', was to be seen through the lace curtains of the front windows of many of the respectable and comfortable homes in his day. Having sold his principles for a piece of common flora, Comstock offered himself small consolation: 'Everyone rebels against the money-code, and everyone sooner or later surrenders.'[6]

While it is true that a lack of money does have its serious drawbacks, Comstock's devotion to money, which is enshrined on the title page of the Secker and Warburg edition of the novel, goes too far:

> Though I speak with the tongues of men and of angels, and have not money, I am become as a sounding brass, or a tinkling cymbal. And though I have the gift of prophecy, and understand all mysteries, and all knowledge; and though I have all faith, so that I could remove mountains, and have not money, I am nothing. And though I bestow all my goods to feed the poor, and though I give my body to be burned, and have not money, it profiteth me nothing. Money suffereth long, and is kind; money envieth not; money vaunteth not itself, is not puffed up, doth not behave unseemly, seeketh not her own, is not easily provoked, thinketh no evil; rejoiceth not in iniquity, but rejoiceth in the truth; beareth all things, believeth all things, hopeth all things, endureth all things ... And now abideth faith, hope, money, these three; but the greatest of these is money.
>
> I Corinthians XIII (*adapted*)

We have to distinguish between the legitimate enjoyment of material things, which the Bible takes for granted and nowhere disputes ('God ... richly provides us with everything for our enjoyment'; 1 Tim. 6:17b), and an illegitimate and unhealthy attachment to wealth as an end in itself ('the love of money is a root of all kinds of evil'; 1 Tim. 6:10a). A number of Christian authors have attempted to draw this distinction. We will review the ideas of three, namely Augustine, David Clarkson and Martyn Lloyd-Jones.

The Church Father Augustine presents an understanding of idolatrous greed in terms of the notions of enjoyment and pleasure. According to Augustine, there is a distinction between those things which are to be enjoyed and those which are to be used: 'To enjoy a thing is to rest with satisfaction in it for its own sake. To use, on the other hand, is to employ whatever means are at one's disposal to obtain what one desires.'[7] The failure to observe this distinction results in sin: 'Every human evil or vice consists in seeking to enjoy things that are to be used, and to use things that are to be enjoyed.'[8] In the strictest sense, only God is to be enjoyed, and things are to be used as means to this end. Sin results when we enjoy things, in the sense of finding true and ultimate joy and satisfaction in them, and use God to procure more and more things. Thus the greedy are clearly guilty of idolatry in that they love money rather than God.

Justo L. González explains this Augustinian perspective: 'The greedy seek to enjoy their possessions and sometimes even to use God in order to increase their wealth. In doing so, they fall into crass idolatry, for only God is to be enjoyed and all things are to be used to attain that enjoyment.'[9]

The Puritan David Clarkson once preached a

sermon in London on the words 'Greed ... is idolatry' in Colossians 5:5, entitled 'Soul idolatry excludes men out of heaven', which is remarkably comprehensive and penetrating. Clarkson distinguishes between two sorts of idolatry: external, involving actions of the body, including bowing and prostrating oneself, which he describes as open and gross idolatry; and internal, consisting of acts of the soul, 'when the mind is most taken up with an object, and the heart and affections most set upon it',[10] which he designates 'secret and soul idolatry'.[11]

Clarkson analyses the worship of the soul in terms of thirteen acts, and charges that 'to give any one of them to anything besides the God of heaven is plain idolatry'.[12] He argues that it is necessary to define clearly the proper worship of God in order to understand the idolatrous worship of the greedy. Ten of these so-called acts of worship develop the concept of the love of money. Indeed, Clarkson makes it clear that for him the heart of the matter is the question of love: 'for wherein does the idolatry of covetousness consist, but in this? That it is an inordinate, an immoderate love of riches.'[13]

The following summary draws on Clarkson's own language: God is, for every human being, that which (1) we most highly value or esteem; (2) we are most mindful of, be it profits and pleasures or God himself; (3) we most intend (our chief aim or purpose), whether to be rich, great and powerful or to glorify God; (4) we are most resolved for, whether lusts and outward advantages or God's ways, honour and service; (5) we most love and adore;[14] (6) we most fear (the loss of); (7) we most desire and enjoy, either worldly enjoyments or 'spiritual communion with God'; (8) we most delight and rejoice in; (9) we are most zealous for, be it our own things or the things of God; and (10) we are most grateful for.

When later in the sermon he lists sixteen ways in which 'men make wealth and riches their god', it is this idea of misplaced affections that he amplifies. Note the following verbs and phrases: the greedy value, love, desire, delight in, grieve over, are more affected by, eagerly seek and prize material things more highly than God.

The breadth of Clarkson's definition of soul idolatry is matched by the size of the net in which he believes the guilty are captured: 'Every natural man, let his enjoyments, privileges, accomplishments, be what they will, is an idolater ... [and] the greatest part of Christians.'[15] Comparing this vast throng to Jacob (in Genesis 31), who denied the presence of idols in his possession, Clarkson asserts that 'though few will own it [soul idolatry], nothing is more common'.[16] This grim diagnosis continues in terms of the corruption of human apprehensions, thoughts, goals, supports, expectations, affections, elections, inclinations and fruitions, through the examination of which Clarkson aims to uncover 'the guilt of this secret sin'.[17]

Finally, the influential twentieth-century Welsh preacher Martyn Lloyd-Jones, although he did not use the terms 'love', 'devotion', 'heart' or 'affections', gave an explanation of 'greed as idolatry' which nevertheless qualifies as a description of the inordinate love of the greedy for their possessions. Its value lies in the fact that the description works well in reverse: what the greedy do with money, they should rather do with God; hence the accusation of idolatry: 'anything that you and I tend to set up as the big thing, the central thing, in our lives, the thing about which we think and dream, the thing that engages our imagination, the thing that we live for, the thing that gives us the biggest thrill, if it is anything other than God, it is idolatry'.[18]

When the Bible condemns the love of money it does not expect us to turn ourselves into glum killjoys; things are to be heartily enjoyed as part of God's good creation. Nor does it call us to stop preferring one food over another (I love seafood and hate corned beef); desire leading to strong personal preference is beside the point. Rather, the love of material things is to be resisted when desire leads to a *consuming quest*. Tragically, many people's lives are characterized by such a quest from the cradle to the grave. What we politely call 'getting something behind us', 'moving up', 'becoming more comfortable' or 'improving our circumstances' is often just a thin disguise for the fact that we are 'in love with this present world' (2 Tim. 4:10, Revised Standard Version).

## The lust of the eyes

The Sermon on the Mount contains an enigmatic saying concerning the soundness of a person's vision: 'The eye is the lamp of the body. So, if your eye is sound, your whole body will be full of light; but if your eye is not sound, your whole body will be full of darkness' (Matt. 6:22–23, Revised Standard Version).

The key term for understanding these words is 'sound', the Greek word *haplous*. It literally means 'single' and is used in the Greek Old Testament as a metaphor for undivided loyalty in the service of God. The point being made is that if you are focused on just one thing, obeying God, you will see where you are going and won't lose your way in life.

A related term is used in the New Testament with the connotation of generosity, and may well be intended here in view of the contrast with 'the evil eye' in verse 23, which can be used to express miserliness and stinginess. Perhaps a double meaning is intended, since both the themes of total devotion to God and detachment from material concerns are treated in the context of verses 19–21 and 24–34. These verses supply a sombre message worth pondering: the greedy will have divided loyalties and won't be able to see where they are going. They live without clear direction or orientation. They don't see things as they really are. Their entire person is in moral darkness.

Human desires are in fact often conceived of as involving the eyes. This is especially the case when the objects of desire involve food or the opposite sex. We chastize children who take too much food by saying that their eyes are bigger than their stomach. And our pupils dilate automatically at the sight of someone we find attractive. If the Bible sometimes describes sexual immorality as 'the lust of the flesh', greed is said to be 'the lust of the eyes' (1 John 2:16, Revised Standard Version). Intriguingly, in Ecclesiastes the Preacher puts these two lusts in close proximity. He claims to have amassed for himself 'silver and gold ... and the treasures of kings and provinces ... and a harem as well, the delights of the heart of man ... I denied myself nothing my eyes desired' (2:8, 10; cf. 4:8).

The link between sexual desire and the desire for riches is well known in our day and frequently exploited in advertising. Marketing for everything from swimming-pools to power tools employs the strategy. Such advertising plays on the viewer's desire to possess both the beautiful model and, by association, the product on display. Indeed, the essence of greed, like lust, is the desire to possess absolutely and exclusively.

Any approach to dealing with the love of money takes this into account. Some religious orders solve the problem by calling on their members to renounce all material possessions. At the other extreme, communism calls for private property to be abolished altogether in favour of state or communal ownership. The problem, however, is not that we as individuals *have* things, but that we hold on to them so tightly. Would you think you had 'lost everything' if in a fire you lost everything? In part, the Bible's solution to the love of money is to help us loosen our grip on our possessions and get a grip on something which far exceeds them in value.

Understandably, people tend to love things of

## Seeing is deceiving

What do I see when I close my eyes?
What precious goal engages my mind?
In secret meditation, what prize
Ensnares my heart, and all senses binds?

Do daydreams distract with things that
   spark
Like icicles, doomed before the sun?
Does unfocused vision seek the dark
Unswervingly, like bullet from gun?

What imagined vault protects my wealth?
What fancied key unlocks its great gate?
Which fell nightmare phantom treads with
   stealth
To steal that horde, and thus seal my
   fate?


Closed or open, where do my eyes gaze?
Can I pretend they find the real light?
Or, more often, groping through the haze,
Sense that seen as evidence of sight?

lasting value. This is true not just of antiques and works of art, but also of cars, furniture, sporting equipment and shoes. Our favourite building materials are usually those that maintain their finish. Cheap materials in time devalue themselves. On the other hand, we condemn as immature our children's attachment to things which obviously will not last, such as fairground toys and the free gimmicks which come with children's fast-food meals. What is the point of loving something that is destined for the rubbish bin?

1 John 2:15–17 applies this logic to all material possessions: 'Do not love the world or anything in the world ... [for] the world and its desires pass away.' Likewise Paul advises 'those who buy something' to live 'as if it were not theirs to keep', and 'those who use the things of the world, as if not engrossed in them ... for this world in its present form is passing away' (1 Cor. 7:30–31). Material things are not the last word. The social and economic institutions which seem so important to us now have no ultimate permanence.

The purest forms of greed are based on a worldview which does not acknowledge the world to come. The prospect of death has an inescapable logic for those who see it as the end of existence: get what you can, while you can. God recommends not world denial, but a recognition, along with the Godgivenness of material things, of their inherent limitation and transience. In view of eternity, even top-drawer merchandise has an inbuilt obsolescence.

## Loving God with your money

The Bible has much to say about love. It has one whole book which celebrates the beauty of love between a man and a woman. It narrates numerous romances, speaks of the love of good food, love of sound teaching and love between brothers and sisters, love for the nation and love for one's children. It also warns against certain kinds of love, including love of sleep, love of the flattering praise of others, and most frequently of all, the love of money. Its main reflections on love are, however, not negative but positive. The Bible commends love for God as the highest, purest, most ennobling and enduring form of love: 'Hear, O Israel: The LORD our God, the LORD is one. Love the LORD your God with all your heart and with all your soul and with *all your strength*' (Deut. 6:4–5, my italics).

Israel's great Shema (as this passage is known), which Jesus referred to as the first and greatest commandment (Mark 12:28–31), and which was read daily (along with the Ten Commandments) in the temple in Jerusalem, receives an unusual rendering in the targums, the Aramaic paraphrases of the Old Testament which were used in the first-century synagogues. They offer a fairly literal translation of Deuteronomy 6, with one striking exception. In verse 5 one targum has: 'Now you should love the Lord your God with your whole heart, and (with your whole) soul, as well as with *all your possessions*' (my italics). The Hebrew 'strength' is rendered by the word 'mammon', which means 'wealth' or 'possessions'. Two other targums use the related term 'money'.[19]

Deuteronomy 6:4–5 expresses God's claim to our ultimate and full allegiance and a refusal to share this loyalty with another. The Lord alone is our creator, redeemer and judge, and as such calls for a total commitment in terms of love. The rest of the chapter in effect elaborates on this demand for exclusive loyalty to God. In this context it is indeed striking that one of the loyalties singled out in early Jewish interpretation as a threat to faithfulness to God concerns wealth and money. Apparently possessions were considered a potent rival which could intrude upon and spoil our love for God. It is not that love for money and material things is somehow evil in and of itself. Rather, it is harmful to us in that it robs us of something far better. If the person 'who loves money will not be satisfied with money' (Eccles. 5:10, Revised Standard Version), the one who loves God will.

# 4
# MISPLACED TRUST

What is the first word that pops into your head when I say 'money'? Many of us are familiar with the psychological test in which a person is confronted with a string of words and must in each case respond immediately with a single word. Supposedly the test can reveal the deep significance which you attach to something. What associations does the word 'money' carry for you?

Money means different things to different people. Money is everything from pleasure, comfort, contentment, freedom and fun, to filth, imprisonment, disgust and degradation. For a great many people money is, above all, security. Fear is a universal human emotion which all of us deal with every day. Fear breeds insecurity. One of the main ways in which we make ourselves secure for the future is by accumulating money. The very language of finance demonstrates this function of money. You can literally buy futures and securities.

There are basically two problems with putting our trust and confidence in money. First, God gets jealous. And secondly, it doesn't work.

## The jealousy of God

In the Bible God is depicted, among other things, as a king. As king, he expects trust and confidence in his ability to provide for and protect his subjects. When the Israelites asked for a king of their own, God took it personally. In response to their request he asserted that 'they have rejected me as their king', and he compared the offence to 'forsaking me and serving other gods' (1 Sam. 8:7–8).

When the nation of Israel felt under threat from hostile neighbouring powers, they did the sensible thing and entered into treaties for the sake of national security. Such treaties, however, were regarded by the prophets as nothing less than unfaithfulness to God. The nation was looking to Egypt or Assyria for help instead of to God. Isaiah chides the nation for her treaty with Egypt along these lines:

> Woe to those who go down to Egypt for help,
>     who rely on horses,
> who trust in the multitude of their chariots
>     and in the great strength of their horsemen,
> but do not look to the Holy One of Israel,

or seek help from the LORD.
… the Egyptians are men and not God.

(31:1–3; cf. Jer. 2:18–19)

Ezekiel compares such treaties to the marital unfaithfulness we normally associate with idolatry: 'You engaged in prostitution with the Egyptians, your lustful neighbours, and provoked me to anger with your increasing promiscuity … You engaged in prostitution with the Assyrians too' (16:26, 28).

The nation was not guilty of literally worshipping other gods, yet they are effectively charged with idolatry for trusting in a substitute for God. Idolatry in this sense is *an attack on God's exclusive rights to our trust and confidence*.

Trust and confidence frequently describe  people's attitude to idols. The Lord describes the idols of the wayward Israelites in Deuteronomy as that in which they take shelter, the rock in which they sought refuge (32:37–38). The idol-worshippers in Isaiah 44:17 say to their idols: 'Save me; you are my god.' And according to Habakkuk 2:18 the one who fashions an idol 'trusts in his own creation'.

Not surprisingly, the Bible accuses the greedy of this same form of idolatry. Psalm 52:7 asserts that the person 'who did not make God his stronghold … trusted in his great wealth'. Proverbs 18:10–11 sets forth the same alternative: 'The name of the LORD is a strong tower; the righteous run to it and are safe. The wealth of the rich is their fortified city; they imagine it an unscalable wall.' And in Proverbs 28:25 a greedy person is contrasted with one who trusts in the Lord. Significantly, in the so-called 'psalms of trust' the two main alternatives to God as objects of trust are idols and riches (see Pss. 115:2–9; 40:4; 62:8–10).

The call to trust in God and not money is also sounded in the New Testament. It is implied in the instructions to the disciples not to take any money with them when they undertake the work of mission (e.g. Mark 6:8–9), and in the calling of Peter and Matthew to leave all and follow Jesus (Mark 1:18–20; Luke 5:28). In 1 Timothy 6:17 the rich are warned straight out to trust not in their riches but in God. The parable of the rich fool in Luke 12:13–34 puts the lesson in the form of a story, and Jesus points to the birds and lilies, both of which trust God for their food and clothing, as examples to follow (Matt. 6:25–34).

Trust and pride often go together. The wicked 'trust in their wealth and boast of their great riches' (Ps. 49:6). What we go to for security and protection is what we boast about. Hence 1 Timothy 6:17 calls the rich not to be arrogant, and in Luke 16:14–15 wealth is 'highly valued among men'. Riches and arrogance are stable partners. The rich often appear to be smug, superior and self-satisfied. God's preference for the humble has to do with their readiness to trust exclusively in him.

No-one in the history of the church placed more importance on the judgment that greed is idolatry, and made more use of it in preaching, Bible exposition and theology, than Martin Luther. The foundation for Luther's understanding of greed as

# The voyage of conviction

Aboard the good ship *Cherished Wealth*
We steer our course with canny stealth.
Our heads held high in measured pride,
Above the waves of need we ride,
Our compass fixed to mortal line,
Our watches set by Western Time.
The journey, threescore years and ten,
Or maybe longer – who knows when
We'll tie up on that distant shore?
It doesn't matter – now is more
Important to the minds of those
Who travel on such trusty boats.
They're made of precious metals, these,
No iceberg feared, no storm can freeze
The hearts of this most gallant crew
Who ride the ship, and built it too.

Our Captain is invincible –
Recruited us when we were small,
Instructed each one day by day,
Impressed on us The Only Way,
Rejected those who showed some doubt,
Infected those who felt left out;
Instilled in us the need to win
(To lose, the unforgiven sin).
He closed our minds to nagging fears;
When conscience spoke he stopped our
    ears.
We learnt our lesson – wealth is might –
And now we're here we know he's right.
You had your chance to jump aboard;
You spoke of God – who needs the Lord?
You're welcome to your pious strife;
Our parting shot, though: get a life!

idolatry is laid in his treatment of the first commandment. What does it mean to have no other gods before the Lord? Luther defines worship broadly in terms of the idea of trust. In the catechisms which Luther wrote to nurture young Christians, he explains how to have no other gods before the Lord: we are to fear, love and trust God above all things. A god is that in which we put our trust and confidence. To obey the first commandment is, according to Luther, to cling to, rely upon and look only to God for whatever we need in any circumstance.

People have as a god that from which they expect to obtain help and comfort. Whereas faith is trust in God's help, unbelief is trust in oneself or one's own powers. In this sense, Luther insisted, unbelief and greed go and grow together. The greater the greed, the more unbelief, and *vice versa*. Sadly, material prosperity is often accompanied by loss of trust in God. The rich often think they simply don't need to trust in God. They have made other arrangements. Like the rich farmer in Jesus' parable ('I will ... build bigger [barns] ... I'll say to myself, "You have plenty of good things laid up for many years. Take life easy"'; Luke 12:18–19), whom he calls a fool, each of us is prone to trust in his or her own resources.

Sin for Luther is always an act of contempt for God. It is significant for Luther that when Moses explains the first commandment, in terms of what causes someone to break it, he first of all mentions riches and luxurious living, which Luther interprets as mammon and greed: 'When the LORD your God brings you into the land … with large, flourishing cities … houses filled with all kinds of good things … and vineyards and olive groves … be careful that you do not forget the LORD' (Deut. 6:10–12). Trusting in riches prevents the human heart from being ruled by faith and love, and consequently the Lord is forgotten. For Luther, Moses himself understood the first commandment in a spiritual sense, as trust in God, and idolatry as a trust in things.

Whereas we uniformly regard some financial gain (be it a promotion, inheritance, profit, or whatever) as an unqualified blessing which cannot fail to put a smile on our face, the Bible contains many warnings which suggest that such windfalls can in effect be a curse. Deuteronomy 8:12–14, for example, indicates that prosperity may lead to pride, self-reliance and forgetting the Lord. Likewise, in Deuteronomy 32:10–15 newly acquired wealth is said to lead to abandoning God: the Lord cared for Israel, gave her the produce of the field, honey, oil, milk, the best cuts of meat and the finest of flour, only to watch the nation grow fat and self-satisfied, and eventually to forsake and scoff at him. Indeed, Proverbs 30:8–9 teaches that it is better to be denied wealth than to be wealthy and deny God: 'Give me neither poverty nor riches … Otherwise I may have too much and disown you, and say, "Who is the LORD?"'

Finally, in Job 31:24–28 both greed and idolatry are understood as involving trust in a substitute for God and are said to constitute unfaithfulness to God. The greedy person, like the idolater, is guilty of misplaced trust. Job explains that if he had made silver and gold his trust or called fine gold his confidence, or if he had committed idolatry by worshipping the sun and the moon, both these sins would have constituted effective denials of the true God.

Many people recognize the dangers which money can pose. Most of us would regard £1 million in cash and an annual income of £250,000 to be a dream come true. 'I could live on that!' might be our wry and knowing response. The fact is that you could also die on it. The Duke and Duchess of Northumberland's son Percy was heading for this lump sum and annual top-up on his eighteenth birthday via a trust set up in 1918 by the seventh Duke of Northumberland. When he reached fourteen years of age the legal guardians of the fund voted unanimously to defer the inheritance until he turns twenty-five. Edward Davidson, the Duke's lawyer, explained that the decision had been taken in Percy's best interest: 'He could harm himself very severely if he has a fund of this size. The Marquess of Bristol inherited a large sum of money on his 21st birthday and never recovered from it.'[1] It is striking that the beneficiary of such 'good fortune' should be described as being in danger of 'very severe harm'. Apparently the marquess to whom the lawyer referred died from what his family described as 'chronic drug abuse'.

## The futility of riches

The problem with being rich and thinking that you don't need God is that you are wrong. The same goes for the person who worships an idol and expects to gain some benefit. Both greed and idolatry are not only wrong, but stupid.

One of the main premisses of the biblical injunction against idolatry is that it is useless. Many pagans believed that certain benefits, such as fertility, rain and health, resulted from worshipping idols. Against this background, many Old Testament texts proclaim the ineffectualness and vanity of idolatry. The Bible ridicules idol worship, portraying it as powerless and deceptive. Such texts stress the perishable nature of the idols, their human origin in the mind and skills of the maker, and their lifelessness.

The worship of idols leads inevitably to the disappointment and embarrassment of those who trust in them. Habakkuk 2:18–19 is just one example:

> Of what value is an idol, since a man has
>     carved it?
>     Or an image that teaches lies?
> For he who makes it trusts in his own
>     creation;
>     he makes idols that cannot speak.
> Woe to him who says to wood, 'Come to life!'
>     Or to lifeless stone, 'Wake up!'
> Can it give guidance?
>     It is covered with gold and silver;
>     there is no breath in it.

Wealth is likewise ultimately unreliable and trust in riches useless. Proverbs asserts that wealth is fleeting and is not a firm basis for security: 'Whoever trusts in his riches will fall' (11:28; cf. 18:11–12). The possibility of imminent death is also linked to the futility of storing up riches (cf. Ps. 49:10–14, 16–17; Prov. 10:2; 27:24; 28:22; Ecc. 15:3–14). In Shakespeare's *Measure for Measure* (III, 1) the Duke says to Claudio:

> If thou art rich, thou'rt poor;
> For, like an ass whose back with ingots bows,
> Thou bear'st thy heavy riches but a journey,
> And death unloads thee.

The fact that some people appreciate this can be seen occasionally today from the bizarre lengths to which the fabulously wealthy sometimes go to try to prolong their lives.

The richest centre of trade in the New Testament period was the city of Rome. The commercial interests of imperial Rome spanned the entire known world. For many under her rule, especially those who were not well off, the city was seen as the ultimate expression of unbridled avarice. And by rich and poor alike, her power was taken to be immense and her rule impregnable. Yet Revelation 18 prophesies the fall of Rome / Babylon, calling to mind the fall of Tyre, the greatest trading centre of the Old Testament period (which is prophesied in Ezek. 26 – 28 and Is. 23). Those who stand to lose most from her demise are the focus of the account, namely, the kings (18:9–10), the merchants (18:11–17a) and (their employees) the seafarers (18:17b–19). These three classes of mourners are precisely the people who benefit directly from Rome's prosperity. They lament their lost merchandise in 18:12–13 ('cargoes of gold, silver, precious stones and pearls; fine linen, purple, silk and scarlet cloth', and so on), the imported luxury goods which represent their crass extravagance. And in 18:14 Rome's self-indulgent opulence, ostentatious display and addiction to consumption are decried: her fruit, dainties and splendour are lost, 'never to be recovered'. Such imagery makes the unreliability of riches abundantly clear.

Jesus pointed to moth, rust and thieves in Matthew 6:19–21 in order to underscore the precariousness of wealth. And the rich are advised in 1 Timothy 6:17 not to trust in the uncertainty of riches (but in the God who alone is immortal).

While death may still be around, some might suggest that money is today a far more stable and reliable form of security than in antiquity. And solutions have surely been found for the proverbial moth and rust! Isn't such talk simply out of date? In short, the answer is no. To think that money can provide security is to be deluded.

Money offers no protection against the vagaries of nature, the so-called acts of God. So many things are out of our hands and can spoil our plans in an instant. Unemployment, war and natural disasters are only the tip of the iceberg. We used to say something was 'as safe as the Bank of England'. Yet the Bank of England has not been entirely successful at bringing economic stability and was powerless to save a bank as prestigious as Barings, for example. Pension funds are likewise not always what they appear. And insurance companies do not always pay up. Lloyds of London, which has the backing of the wealthy Names, seemed impregnable. Yet in the eighteen months prior to the meeting in the Albert Hall to discuss the crisis which threatened to undo Lloyds, thirty Names had taken their lives, in despair over their financial demise.

Natural disasters such as hurricanes, earthquakes, floods and tidal waves seem to be ever more frequent in our day. The north and south polar ice-caps are melting. The ozone layer is disintegrating. Major earthquakes and volcanic eruptions are expected in numerous densely populated areas. World population is exploding. And terrorists are becoming better armed. Such developments make the moth, rust and thieves of which Jesus spoke look pretty harmless when it comes to the threats they potentially pose to our possessions.

Another problem with seeking security through material acquisition is that other people notice our wealth, and the cost of security tends to spiral. Envy can lead to burglary and theft. The fear of such things leads many rich people to live in what amount to fortresses. Security without freedom is a good definition of incarceration.

Trust in wealth is, in the final analysis, a sad example of human folly. But worse than that, it is an insult to the Creator and Sustainer of the universe, who alone constitutes the sure ground for our confidence and trust.

# 5
# FORBIDDEN SERVICE

In the ancient world the institution of slavery was taken for granted. Most religions, including Judaism and early Christianity, employed the model of 'servant and master' to talk about how to relate to God. Few people questioned the assumption that almost everybody served somebody or other, whether God, one of the pagan gods or a human master. In the modern world, by contrast, we congratulate ourselves on the abolition of slavery and we prize our personal freedom. Slavery is thankfully a thing of the past. Or is it?

## Unintentional servitude

In the Old Testament, a primary action of believers towards God, and of idolaters towards their gods, was service and obedience. Even in ceremonial contexts, the notion of serving the deity signified more than just isolated acts of cultic worship. When it is said that people served one of the gods such as Baal, or the Lord, the term implied not only the exclusive nature of the relationship but the total commitment and obedience of the worshipper. That worship involved service in the sense of submission to the will of a higher authority is clear from the phrase 'to bow the knee', which is used by Paul as a synonym for worship (Rom. 11:4; 14:11; Eph. 3:14; Phil. 2:10).

Thus it is something of a puzzle when we read the words of Jesus which claim that some people serve money (Matt. 6:24; Luke 16:13). How is that possible? Some have suggested that Jesus was referring to a demon or god. In the nineteenth century a few scholars claimed that Mammon was a known Syrian deity, and in some post-apostolic Christian sources Mammon is depicted as the demon of wealth. Certainly Jesus believed in the existence of the Evil One and his cohorts, whose goal it is to tempt humans to disobey God. There is no convincing first-century evidence, however, for a firm link between greed and a demon or god. A better explanation is that Jesus' words, 'You cannot serve both God and Money' (Matt. 6:24), personify wealth as an evil and superhuman power which distracts people from serving the true God. It was a well-known insight not only among Jesus and Christians, but also among Greeks and Romans in general, that wealth could exercise an enslaving power.

No-one sets out to become a slave of money, and most people do not recognize their servitude until it is too late. People wrongly assume that money is serving them. Several authors have noticed this cruel irony. The Church Father Cyprian (died 258), Bishop of Carthage, wrote of those

> who add forests to forests, and who, excluding the poor from their neighbourhood, stretch out their fields far and wide into space without limits ... Such a one enjoys no security either in his food or in his sleep. In the midst of the banquet he sighs, although he drinks from a jewelled goblet; and when his luxurious bed has enfolded his body, languid with feasting, he lies wakeful in the midst of the down; nor does he perceive, poor wretch, that these things are merely gilded torments, that he is *held in bondage* by his gold, and that he is the *slave* of his luxury and wealth rather than their master.[1]

The English philosopher and lawyer Francis Bacon (1561–1626) agreed: 'If money be not thy servant, it will be thy master. The covetous man cannot so properly be said to possess wealth, as that may be said to possess him.'[2] And the French theologian and ethicist Jacques Ellul stated: 'We can, if we must, use money, but it is really money that uses us and makes us servants by bringing us under its law and subordinating us to its aims.'[3]

The tragic and pitiful figure of Ebenezer Scrooge,

in *A Christmas Carol* by Charles Dickens, represents well the slavery which greed imposes. In an encounter concocted by the Ghost of Christmas Past, Scrooge is confronted with the awful truth that he worships a golden idol: 'I have seen your nobler aspirations fall off one by one, until the master-passion, Gain, engrosses you.' As a younger man 'there was an eager, greedy, restless motion in the eye, which showed the passion that had taken root, and where the shadow of the growing tree would fall'.[4] To his surprise, it is made clear to Scrooge that what he needs is nothing short of 'release' from his captivity.

A nineteenth-century hymn by Joseph Barnby tells the story of the Macedonian man's cry for help (Acts 16:9–10), a vision Paul received on his second missionary journey to take the gospel from Asia Minor into Europe. Whereas the first two verses expand the call taking Macedonia as a symbol for fallen humanity (for example, 'How mournfully it echoes on!/For half the earth is Macedon;/These brethren to their brethren call/... "O ye that live, behold we die!"'), the third verse takes pains to stress that, paradoxically, the world as a whole neither issues nor hears the call. 'By other sounds the world is won/Than that which wails from Macedon.' According to the hymn, the world 'cannot list the alien cry'. The cause of people's indifference to their need of God is put down to greed: 'The roar of gain is round it [the world] rolled,/Or men unto themselves are sold.' Not only does the clamour for more drown out the cry from Macedon, but humans are depicted as in bondage to these very lusts.

## Serving Mammon

Slavery to money can affect those at every level of society, and may even be thought of as encompassing society as a whole. It has its grip on people at every socio-economic level. But worst of all, it can cause people to act in hard, unfeeling and even self-destructive ways, as the Church Father John Chrysostom brought out in his frequent references to the judgment that greed is idolatry.[5]

Chrysostom explained the equation in terms of forbidden service. Above all, Chrysostom felt the shocking rhetorical impact of the words and sought with all earnestness to impress them upon his hearers. He insists that to call greed idolatry is no exaggeration, but in fact 'pure truth'. Greed, according to Chrysostom, is 'an illness of the soul', 'the worst type of decay'. He expects his hearers to 'shiver' and 'shudder' at Paul's words and to 'flee from this decay and seize the imperishable'. With 'preacher's licence' he goes as far as to say that greed is 'worse than idolatry'; the greedy person is 'much worse than an idolater' because, whereas idolaters defend their form of worship, the greedy happily condemn in others the thing they themselves worship.

Chrysostom believed that the greedy are guilty of idolatry because they serve and obey something other than God. Anticipating the objection of the greedy that they do not worship their money, he counters: 'Do you deny it [the charge of idolatry] because you do not kneel in front of it? You are bowing much lower before it by your works, and that constitutes greater servility. In order to recognize this, look upon God and tell me: Who worships him more? Those who only stand praying before him or those who do his will? Obviously the latter. Thus those who do his will, serve mammon more diligently.'

For Chrysostom, the fact that the greedy serve their own selfish desires comes out in several ways. He claims that the 'altar of greed … strongly smells of human blood', implying that the greedy oppress the poor and needy in their relentless drive for more. With reference to Cain, who 'wanted to cheat God due to greed', he explains that greed leads to a lack of love, and eventually to pride and even 'hatred and contempt of fellow human beings'. The unstated premiss in Chrysostom's interpretation is that since greed demands behaviour that involves disobedience to God, then such service involves 'falling away from God' and thus may justifiably be called idolatry. In order to lead the greedy to repentance, he stresses the goodness of God in creation in supplying human needs and 'an inheritance in heaven', a far superior form of riches (a strategy we will explore in chapter 8).

One of the great problems with money is that the more you earn the more you spend. If you ask people how much is enough, most of us, if we are honest, will answer, 'Just a bit more.' No matter where we are on the salary scale, people tend to look enviously upon those just above them. What we forget is that those people do the same thing with the ones on the rung above, and so it goes on.

Those who do, by all accounts, earn enough are often trapped in work that harms their quality of life. Why is it that people stay in jobs which clearly damage their health, their general well-being and their families? The answer is they are in slavery. They simply cannot accept a job on lower pay, because people, naturally enough, match their lifestyle to their income. And it does not take long to get used to a better income. Most people literally could not afford to accept a lower income.

Family therapists report that, when counselling families in need, you can ask the adults to consider the way they are treating each other, how they relate to the children, and so on. Such questions usually evoke little resistance. If you ask whether an adult needs to work so long and hard or might consider a different job, however, the responses range from intransigence to incredulity. Consider the experience of one counsellor:

> I was talking to a guy recently – he and his wife were having troubles with their daughter – we talked about that and that was fine, and then we were talking about what the difficulties were and that was fine, and we were getting on and then it came around to how much of the problem was dad, and dad was working fifteen hours a day, seven days a week. People were ringing him up in the middle of

the night and things like that. He looked physically ill. He said, 'It's just the work', and I said, 'Well, can't you cut it down? It doesn't look to be doing you much good.' He said, 'Yes, but I've got to keep going at it.' I said, 'What if you just say that's it, forget it, I'm going somewhere else.' He said, 'I did that last year and they just put my pay up by 25 per cent and how do you walk away from that?'[6]

Such a tale does seem to approximate to a modern form of slavery. It is indeed a rare person who can make a decision which reduces his or her income. Many of us are slaves rather than masters when it comes to our money.

In the light of this, and in order to understand such self-destructive behaviour, it is tempting to conceive of greed as an addiction. Addiction is among the most tragic things that can happen to you or a loved one.[7] Whereas the pleasures gained from drugs and alcohol are seldom denied, those who become addicted to such substances can find themselves and those around them in deep despair. In a society that teaches that we are our own creators, there are few more frightening scenarios than losing control of oneself. From all appearances, the addict is bound by a pattern of destructive behaviour laced with obsession and delusion.

The dynamics of addiction are well known. What starts out as a pleasant habit escalates to a point where decidedly unpleasant after-effects lead to deteriorating relationships and withdrawal from worthwhile activities. Preoccupation leads to obsession and compulsive behaviour; excuses lead to denials, delusions and self-deception. Others are drawn into the web of addiction to support and enable, perhaps unwittingly, the whole debilitating process. Finally, the addict can truthfully say that there is no choice; the addiction is in charge.

Addiction is a syndrome which gives us an insight into what can happen with so-called appetitive sins like lust, gluttony and, in particular, greed. It would be an exaggeration to label greed an addiction. It may be fair to say, however, that addiction is greed with the volume turned up. Much of what is true about the spiral of addiction could, to a lesser degree, be said of those who create and resent the bondage of greed. Many could identify with the addict's sense of confinement, futility and lack of choice, when it comes to money matters. As minor addictions go, greed is able to injure and disfigure in frightening ways.

Some secular analysts have made observations of the economic behaviour of entire societies which basically amount to the accusation that all of us suffer under a form of economic slavery. In offering his comprehensive critique of capitalism, Karl Marx at one point employs the rhetoric of idolatry. His reflections are not, of course, concerned with the interpretation of the New Testament. We don't normally look to Marx for help in understanding the Bible. In fact, in his discourse the counterpoint to idolatry is not the true worship of God, but rather human self-fulfilment. Nevertheless, what he says

constitutes an unwitting interpretation of the words
'Greed ... is idolatry' which extends Chrysostom's
ideas from the level of the individual to the whole of
society.

Marx reflects on the irony of the capitalist system,
as he saw it, wherein, instead of products belonging
to their producers, the reverse state of affairs obtains,
and alienation results. Products are no longer valued
for their usefulness, but only for their market value.
Money becomes the alien god that confers this value:
'Money is the general, self-sufficient value of
everything. Hence it has robbed the whole world, the
human world as well as nature, of its proper worth.
Money is the alienated essence of man's labor and
life and this alien essence dominates him as he
worships it.'[8]

Marx asserted that greed has a dehumanizing
effect: 'The more the worker exerts himself, the more
powerful becomes the alien objective world which he
fashions against himself, the poorer he and his inner
world become, the less there is that belongs to him.'[9]
In Marx's view, greed is a god because it dominates
people's lives and demands an obedience tantamount
to slavery. Marx views greed not as a matter of
individual morality but as a structural and societal ill.
We do not need to subscribe to his political ideas to
see the disturbing kernel of truth in what Marx says.

Why is greed such a powerful urge that people
and whole communities are taken over by it, to the
extent that they end up serving and obeying money?
It has to do with placing too high a value on material
things. People use money to bolster their sense of

# A short history of bondage

On a green and pleasant planet deep within
　the Milky Way
A pair of foolish creatures sought to make their
　mark one day,
Deciding that the one and only thing they
　weren't to grab
Was worth the risk of losing all the rest of
　what they had.
They suffered for their selfish greed. Forced
　out of Paradise,
Exchanging Eden's corn for desert thorns, they
　paid the price.
Now slaves to their ambition, when once heirs
　to God they'd been,
They parented a human race inheriting their
　schemes,
Who, not content with Providence, built gods of
　gold instead,
And worshipped the creation rather than
　creation's Head.
And though that God sent his dear Son to
　show them how to live,
They killed him. They preferred to take – they
　did not want to give.
And still they build their gilded halls, in truth
　but catacombs,
Where, deep 'neath heaven's fertile soil hell's
　moth and rust consume.
In chains of their own making, fashioned to
　their own design,
They trade eternal freedom just to worship that
　called 'mine'.

existence. In short, to recall the previous two chapters, when it comes to money, many of us suffer from inordinate love and misplaced trust. What is needed is a different way of thinking about ourselves and a new appreciation for the things which are not seen. More will be said on this in the next three chapters.

## Slaves of sin

Both in much theology and in the popular mind, sin is thought of in terms of guilt. The solution to sin is, then, forgiveness. This is of course right and proper. It tells only part of the story, however – one third, to be exact. Sin is not only guilt but also ignorance and a power. God solves all three problems for us sinners through the death and resurrection of Jesus Christ.

What did the cross achieve? First, the cross saves sinners, dealing with our guilt (Rom. 5:1–11). Jesus bore the penalty for our sins so that we might be forgiven and have a right standing with God. Secondly, the cross tells us about God, dealing with our ignorance. At the cross we learn of God's strict justice (Rom. 3:21–26) and amazing love (Rom. 5:8). Thirdly, the cross conquers evil, dealing with our bondage and impotence: through the cross God 'disarmed the powers and authorities' and 'made a public spectacle of them, triumphing over them' (Col. 2:15).

It is this third aspect of sin and salvation that is often neglected and has keen relevance to the forbidden service of money. Sin blinds and binds.

We need not only forgiveness and true knowledge of God but liberation and deliverance, which is what the word 'salvation' really means. But we can't begin to experience this freedom until we acknowledge our bondage. Too many of us are so busy making ends meet that we fail to notice the chains that bind us. The Germans have a saying: 'Money is a good slave, but a bad master.'

# 6
# LEARNING CONTENTMENT

Almost everyone agrees that contentment is a good thing. The attractions and benefits of the contented state are obvious. Not to be content is a virtual synonym of unhappiness. And to say, 'I am content', is as positive an assessment of a situation as many people are ever willing to give. Indeed, the person experiencing the highest bliss can be described as 'filled to his or her heart's content'. To be content is to be satisfied, to enjoy a balance between one's desires and their fulfilment. To be content is in effect to experience freedom from want.

Whether you are content is more important to your well-being than how well-off you are. The Puritan Jeremiah Burroughs quaintly illustrated this point with reference to the activity of walking. He compared one's heart and one's material possessions to a person's two legs. How well you walk depends less on the length of your legs than on their being even in length. The person with two short legs is far better off than someone with one long leg (being rich and powerful) and one even longer leg (having a proud and insatiable heart).[1]

The fact that contentment is the opposite of greed and the solution to it is clear from the admonition in Hebrews 13:5: 'Keep your lives free from the love of money.' How, we might ask? The verse continues: 'be content with what you have'.

These six words form one of the most difficult commands in the Bible, especially in our day of ingrained consumerism and unquestioned materialism. The world's approach to achieving contentment is by way of addition. 'If only I could get such and such, then I would be satisfied,' or so we tell ourselves. We are like the child who climbs a hill and sees a higher one in the distance, and thinks that from there it will be possible to touch the clouds. Once on top of that hill, we discover that we are just as far from the clouds as before. 'The world is infinitely deceived in thinking that contentment lies in having more than we already have.'[2]

But how are we expected to keep our wants in check when the economy to which we belong is driven by efforts to contrive new wants and dress them up as needs? Since the Second World War, succeeding generations in the West have accommodated their material expectations to what they have attained, whether in terms of the size of their dwellings, their luxuries and appliances, or the money they spend on leisure pursuits like overseas holidays.

To limit yourself voluntarily is a modern-day heresy, which, if discovered, is greeted with bemusement if not disbelief. The mortgage lender finds it hard to fathom a customer who does not apply for the maximum loan permitted by the size of his or her annual income. Virtually no-one is satisfied with what he or she has; few willingly forgo what they could afford. 'Enough' is always just over the horizon, and the horizon recedes as we approach it. To switch metaphors, so many of us are like the caged hamster running furiously in the wheel and getting nowhere, 'trapped in the endless cycle of work and spend, whose poles mutually reinforce each other'.[3]

Like greed, contentment is not only an intensely practical matter which can affect the way we live our lives almost every day, but one which has a profound theological basis and implications.

## Contentment and knowing God

The Christian approach to contentment, like the Christian approach to virtually every subject, begins with the knowledge of God. The Christian faith supplies three good reasons to be content: first, because God himself is content; secondly, because he promises his people a secure future; and thirdly, because we can trust his goodness.

# Animal crackers

When I wake in the morning
He's sleeping on my bed.
When I lie there, still yawning
He doesn't raise his head.
When my mind starts to work on
The worries of the day,
Then my dog shows no symptoms
Of having thoughts that way.

When I've shuffled into clothes,
Dragged a brush through my hair,
And done some more things that show
That there's no time to spare,
Then he crashes off the bed,
Four feet flat on the floor,
And like Laz'rus from the dead
He goes leaping outdoors.

Before the coffee's ready
He's barking to come in;
Doesn't mind that he's dirty –
He's thinking just one thing;
And when the biscuits are gone
Then he's back in his bed,
The morning's work forgotten –
The daydreaming ahead.

While I'm eating my breakfast
I'm thinking 'bout the bills,
Wond'ring who I should pay first
And who might owe *me* still;

Thinking 'bout the new windows
And next month's trip to Greece.
I'm chewing on my fingers
While the dog snores in peace.

I'm pouring out more coffee
While my thoughts are elsewhere –
I'm building a new study,
My brand new private lair.
I'm dreaming of the gismos
That could clutter my desk;
And the box full of biros
For writing out the cheques.

I'm looking at his basket:
The only thing he owns –
Takes no time to look after
The place that he calls home.
If I mention possessions
You will not hear a bark –
Mine cause *him* no congestion;
He can see in the dark.

I'm looking there, still wond'ring,
While searching for my keys –
Which doesn't stop me pond'ring
This scene of canine ease;
And I think I might discern
A smile across his face,
As in bliss he considers
His dog's life, my rat race.

## God's contentment

As odd as it sounds, there is a sense in which God is the contented God. He does not go for everything he can get. We are so used to talking about his infinite knowledge, power and presence that we often forget that in creating and in redeeming us he limited himself in acts of extraordinary self-control. We are not pantheists, believing that God is everything, but theists, holding that God has created and sustains the world but is independent of it. In doing so, the infinite God restricted himself in order to give a measure of freedom to his creatures.[4] Furthermore, he could have gone on creating, but instead stopped after six days.

Likewise, Christ, in becoming a human being, 'emptied himself, taking the very nature of a servant' (Phil. 2:7). As Paul explains, 'though he was rich, yet for your sakes he [voluntarily] became poor' (2 Cor. 8:9). Along with praising God for his infinity, then, we do well to remember his humility.

God takes the lead in self-limitation. And in asking us to be content, he is no hypocrite. Since God was willing to limit himself, we should be ready to follow his example. When he calls us to 'be content with what you have', he cannot help but shake his head in disappointment when we steadfastly refuse his advice. We entirely fail to appreciate the point of view from which it was issued. He is not like the medieval baron who expects his serfs to be satisfied with dry bread, while all the time he himself sups on the finest cuisine and has not the faintest inkling of what it means to do without.

## God's promised future

A proven way to put up with uncomfortable restrictions is to set your mind on your wonderful destination. I am convinced that this is the only way people on long-haul flights are able to bear their many hours of intense discomfort. The same is true of Christians who willingly put up with less than they could afford or with less than they would like to have. Limitations can be borne, if it is clear that they are not permanent.

To cite an extreme example, it is reported that some of the early Christian martyrs found contentment in their sufferings using this logic: 'Though we have but a hard breakfast, yet we shall have a good dinner, [for] we shall very soon be in heaven.'[5]

In a similar fashion, Paul considers his 'light and momentary troubles' to be far outweighed by 'an eternal glory' being prepared for him (2 Cor. 4:17). Paul's troubles, which included imprisonments, days adrift at sea, sleepless nights, cold and exposure (2 Cor. 11:25–27), to mention only his travelling accommodation, were neither light nor momentary by any other measure. Christ was able to bear even the pain and shame of the cross 'for the joy set before him' (Heb. 12:2).

In all these cases the restrictions were entirely voluntary and avoidable. The martyrs could have opted for a better 'breakfast' (by denying Christ), Paul for more salubrious quarters (by sticking to his trade) and Christ for heavenly glory (by forgoing the cross). Christians are uniquely able to be content; as Jeremiah Burroughs put it, 'they see heaven before them and that contents them'.[6]

Or it ought to. It should at least take the edge off our yearning for more now, and ease our disappointment at what we take to be material limitations in the present.

The ultimate incentive to contentment is the confidence that God is on our side and is looking after us. The injunction in Hebrews 13:5 backs up its call to contentment with the words, 'because God has said, "Never will I leave you; never will I forsake you."' In the original Greek these words of comfort from God include no fewer than five negatives; they could hardly be more emphatic. We might paraphrase them: 'I will never, ever, under any circumstances ... fail to be there for you.' He will stick around no matter what happens.

Christians may be content because we have God. Burroughs explains:

> A godly heart enjoys much of God in everything he has, and knows how to make up all wants in God himself ... The saints in heaven do not have houses, and lands, and money, and meat and drink, and clothes; you will say, they do not need them – why not? It is because God is all in all to them immediately.[7]

No matter what the material circumstances on earth,

such a heart can say to itself, 'The LORD is my portion' (Lam. 3:24). God is worth more than anything the world can offer. This is surely what Paul had in mind when he says that he has 'learned to be content … through him who gives me strength' (Phil. 4:11, 13). As the old saying goes, 'It's not where you live that matters, it's who you live with.'

## God's goodness

Contentment is rooted in trust in the goodness of God. As Christians we believe that God knows best how to order things and that he has our best interests at heart. We affirm the universality and comprehensive nature of God's providence. Nothing takes him by surprise or escapes his notice. He knows all about us and is always with us. This does not exempt us from working hard and attempting to improve our lot. But it ought to give us a quietness of spirit to accept our circumstances when things don't turn out as we had hoped.

If we truly believe that God is good, we ought to make a favourable interpretation of his dealings with us. It is a tiresome friend who takes everything you say and do the wrong way and is always looking for fault. A good friend is someone who believes in you and thinks the best of you even when appearances may at times indicate otherwise. We owe God such friendship. Do you feel that you are missing out in some material sense? If you have a clear conscience as regards your own laziness and wrongdoing, and you are left only to turn to comfort in God's will, hold fast to your confession that he knows what he is doing. It is worth remembering that to be given up to your heart's desires may be a dreadful thing (Ps. 81:11–12; Rom. 1:24, 26, 28). Perhaps he is preparing you for some work of service, or is saving you from some temptation that would destroy you. Perhaps he knows that you would not in fact be 'better off' if you were better off.

## The value of contentment

Contentment is in no sense an isolated issue, but is intimately bound up with a host of virtues and vices. It can save a person from a multitude of sins and sets off a chain reaction of blessing that keeps on running.

Contentment requires patience. This applies both to waiting for the life to come and to living sensibly in this life. We don't have the house, the car, the computer or the clothes we want, or whatever it may be, often because we are waiting for some improvement in our circumstances. The real tragedy of being discontented is that in longing for what we don't have, we cease to take pleasure in what we do have. We become frustrated at the child who refuses a nourishing and tasty breakfast cereal just because the box containing his or her favourite is empty. All too often, adults mimic this childish behaviour, albeit in more sophisticated ways. A Jewish rabbi wisely stated: 'Who is rich? He who rejoices in his portion.'[8]

Unfortunately, patience is surprisingly difficult to

achieve. When Paul prays for the Colossians to be 'strengthened with all power according to his glorious might' (1:11), it is not so that they may perform some superhuman feat, but so that they may have the least impressive and most mundane of all the virtues, namely, 'patience'. In a Bible study, the group was asked which of the fruit of the Spirit (Gal. 5:22–23) they needed the most help with; to a person, they all settled on patience.

When preaching on contentment, the Puritan Thomas Manton rightly observed that 'patience is rooted in humility, but discontent in pride'.[9] It is when we think we deserve better that we become discontented. From company executives to visiting professors, whether it concerns free accommodation or complimentary meals, the level of complaint concerning their quality and speed of delivery, which is very often high, is a fair measure of their pride.

By contrast, it is when we consider that 'God has dealt graciously with me', giving me more than I actually deserve, that we can say with Jacob (who said this when he was faced with a decision that would cost him materially), 'I have enough' (Gen. 33:10). Those who think more highly of themselves than they ought find it hard to say, 'Enough.'

Just as discontentment gives off the scent of pride, it reeks of ingratitude. Grumbling is regarded in Scripture as nothing less than rebellion against God. Such attitudes are simply inappropriate for Christians who profess to be dead to the world's fading allurements and alive to the eternal God, whose lives do not consist of their material possessions but are hidden with Christ in God (Col. 3:3). It is no accident that Paul's exposition of what this implies for our lives on earth reaches its pinnacle in a threefold call to give thanks: 'be thankful ... sing ... songs with gratitude in your hearts to God ... whatever you do, whether in word or deed, do it all in the name of the Lord Jesus, giving thanks to God the Father through him' (Col. 3:15–17). Our contentment arises not from getting the things which we want, but from God's fashioning our spirits to our condition and from our recognizing his gracious provision, both spiritual and material.

The modern western worldview, ever since the Enlightenment, has been constructed in individualistic terms. Since capitalism promotes the unrestrained drive for personal increase, this by definition waters down any sense of community – which causes a myriad social problems. Whereas the successful entrepreneur is often proud to stand alone, the essential nature of God is in relationships, both between Father, Son and Spirit in the Trinity and with human beings. The great theologian Karl Barth considered the notion of relationship to be central to the very idea of humans' being created in the image of God: 'male and female he created them' (Gen. 1:27).[10]

If people are going to relate, they have to limit themselves. This applies as much to members of a household, or to castaways on a desert island, as it does to members of a society and even to the world community. When God supplied his people with manna in the wilderness, he instructed them to collect only their share and no more, 'an omer for each person you have in your tent' (Exod. 16:16). This limitation was to prevent some from going hungry because of others' greed, a principle endorsed by Paul in the context of the Corinthian Christians' contribution to the collection for the poor saints in Jerusalem (2 Cor. 8:15). The Lord Jesus taught us to pray, 'Give us today our daily bread' (Matt. 6:11), not 'Give us today enough to hoard for many days to come.'

Limitation for the sake of relationship is also the obvious motivation for the Bible's controversial prohibitions on lending at interest.[11] For us, interest is a legitimate payment for servicing a transaction which empowers someone to buy something now rather than later. Nothing could be more natural and convenient. Yet Deuteronomy 23:19–20 ('Do not charge your brother interest') and Luke 6:35 ('Lend … without expecting to get anything back') take a radically different view. If Old Testament teaching was intended to protect the poor and vulnerable in the Israelite community (the Israelites could exact interest from foreigners), Jesus' instructions transcend the distinction between brother and foreigner, being set in the context of loving one's enemy, doing good and lending with a generous spirit (see Luke 6:32–36).

The terms used for 'interest' tell a story of their own. The Old Testament has three words in Hebrew, which don't shrink from calling a spade a spade: *nešek*, which derives from the word for 'serpent' and means 'bite', refers to the paying of interest from the debtor's point of view; and *marbît* and *tarbît*, meaning 'increase', which see the transaction from the angle of the creditor. The Old Testament forbids 'biting' a fellow-Israelite in order to add to one's stockpile (to risk an unappetizing mixed metaphor). By contrast, we have invented a more civilized and wholly positive term for debt, namely 'credit'.

Some parts of the world see interest in an entirely different light. In 1985 a Brazilian labour leader referred to interest as a weapon more deadly than the atom bomb.[12] Third World debt puts the lie to the essential amorality of lending at interest. Without questioning the altruism of the World Bank, the IMF and the banks of the First World nations, it is no exaggeration to say that many nations today bear tremendous burdens due to their obligations to pay interest on the money they owe. For example, fully one third of Tanzania's budget each year goes on paying its loans. Whether or not empowerment was the intention, these loans have led to the very opposite.

We must, of course, tread carefully in applying the Bible's teaching on usury to our own day. It referred originally to simple lending and borrowing in agrarian communities. Changed economic conditions can't be ignored.[13] At the very least, these texts embody the principle of being satisfied with getting less than one could, for the sake of others.

Indeed, contentment is the essential prerequisite for giving. It is a common fallacy to think that my ability to give hangs more on how much I earn than on my state of contentment. No matter how much I earn there will always be something to spend it on, unless at some point I am satisfied with what I already have. Money will always be in short supply, if I am not content.

When we are content, we exercise faith, humility, love, patience, wisdom and hope. Contentment prepares us to receive mercy and to undertake acts of service. It delivers us from an abundance of temptations. If greed is a hideous sin, contentment is a supreme grace which honours and pleases God.

## Satisfied pigs?

Yet it is possible to have too much of a good thing. When it comes to contentment, this is definitely the case. As one author in the seventeenth century put it, 'many are contented out of mere stupidity'.[14] What they want matches what they have simply because they lack ambition or imagination. It is hard to argue with John Stuart Mill, who famously wrote: 'It is better to be a dissatisfied Socrates than a satisfied pig.'[15]

Just as contentment does not rule out ambition, but rather only the selfish and consuming variety, so too it precludes grumbling, not crying out to God for relief from genuine financial distress. Burroughs conceded: 'Though a Christian ought to be quiet under God's correcting hand, he may without any breach of Christian contentment complain to God.'[16] There is nothing commendable or spiritual in being satisfied in a monetary situation which does your dependants harm, if there is something which can be done about it. Christians are to be content, yet resourceful and hard-working, not indolent or irresponsible.

A second and even more squalid form of inappropriate contentment also involves taking it to an extreme. Christians ought to be at one and the same time the most contented and yet dissatisfied people in the world, for they want something this world cannot offer:

> Godliness teaches us this mystery, Not to be satisfied with all the world for our portion, and yet to be content with the meanest condition in which we are ... A little in this world will content a Christian for his passage, but all the world, and ten thousand times more, will not content a Christian for his portion.[17]

Ultimately, we are not satisfied to wallow in the mire, no matter how resigned to it we might appear. We long for a truly better place (and I don't mean the nicer part of town!). Our hearts are to be set on things above, not on the things of the earth.

# 7
# SHARING POSSESSIONS

Most people in our society tend to regard giving as a purely private business and approach it with the utmost care and the strictest calculation. Whereas we might spontaneously splash out on something special for ourselves when shopping, tight reins are kept on the sober activity of sharing our possessions. And few of us think of our enhanced ability to give when, on those rare but memorable occasions, news of a hefty pay rise brightens up our day. For most of us, giving is an ideal opportunity to exercise rigorous self-control and restraint. 'What's mine is mine' is so obvious that it hardly seems worth saying.

Giving and contentment are two sides of the same coin. Together they represent the positive alternative to greed. If contentment calls a halt to the *grabbing* dimension of greed, giving addresses its *keeping* aspect. Like contentment, giving turns out to be far more central and significant to Christian living and identity than might first appear. In this chapter we will consider not the practicalities of giving, which vary enormously between individuals and cultures, but the centrality of giving in the fight against greed. In order to accomplish this task we will, among other things, need to take a close look at the meaning of some key New Testament words and concepts, including 'greed', 'hospitality' and 'almsgiving'.

## Identifying the greedy

Good detective novels or television series are often hugely popular, perhaps because so many of us enjoy the challenge of sorting through the suspects and picking out the guilty party. If the crime were greed, though, how would we go about pinning the blame?

Who then are the greedy? The problem with defining the word 'greed' in the New Testament is that the relevant words appear mainly in lists of sins to be avoided, which supply little context or clue to their meaning. Naturally enough, commentaries and lexicons seek to give the words a meaning which justifies their appearance alongside the likes of 'murder', 'treachery', 'wickedness' and 'workers of evil', as in Romans 1:28–30, for instance. 'Wanting to get rich, avarice', simply doesn't seem wicked enough, at least to modern western sensibilities. Hence definitions often include the adjective 'ruthless' and associate the concept of greed with dishonesty, violence and oppression. Thus people can be accused of greed only when their behaviour entails hurting others or compromising their integrity.

Simply wanting more wealth, however, was considered a vice by early Jews and Christians, and there were other words which carried the stronger meanings. The fact that 'greed' can signify just wanting to get rich, irrespective of the means employed, is suggested by the existence of Christian teaching which condemns just that: 'Be on your guard against all kinds of greed' (Luke 12:15); 'Do not store up for yourselves treasures on earth' (Matt. 6:19); 'People who want to get rich fall into temptation and a trap' (1 Tim. 6:9).

One place in the New Testament where 'greed' appears in an illuminating context is Luke 12, where the parable of the rich fool gives no indication that the greed being condemned involves anything other than the accumulation of wealth by legitimate means (his land 'produced a good crop'). There are no firm grounds to conclude that greed is condemned only when it leads to other sins, as convenient as it might be to imagine otherwise. This seems to make the task of identifying the greedy unwieldy, to say the least. How many of us do not want to get rich? (You are, after all, reading this book!)

So far, I have suggested that the greedy are those who love money inordinately (chapter 3), trust money excessively (chapter 4), serve money slavishly (chapter 5) and are never satisfied with their possessions (chapter 6). These four definitions could leave the impression that greed is at worst a personal and private sin, which is difficult to recognize in others. Love and trust, for instance, are among the most secret of emotions, to which others have little access without our consent. You might think that I am acting out of love for someone or trust in something, but you could be seriously mistaken.

While we may be accustomed to thinking of greed as a private and intangible vice, this was apparently not the case for the early church. The list of offenders in 1 Corinthians 5:10–11, who are to be excluded from the congregation, includes perpetrators of five very public and concrete offences, namely the sexually immoral person, the idolater, the slanderer, the drunkard and the swindler. There would be plenty of witnesses to pick this lot out of a line-up. The behaviours which characterize them were for the most part public and social. By definition, you can't be a slanderer or a swindler without involving someone else. But, the list also includes the greedy person, who presumably was just as visible and identifiable as the other five. Otherwise there would have been little point in including this offender in the list. How was the greedy person to be recognized?

We may surmise that the greedy in the early church were those who refused to 'do good ... to the family of believers' (Gal. 6:10; cf. 1 John 3:17), or believers who did not share their food with those who had less to eat at the community meals (1 Cor. 11:20–22). In the early church the greedy were probably identified in the first instance as *those who refused to share their possessions.*

## The acquisitor's creed

I believe in Gold, Treasure Almighty, basis of fortune on earth:

And in Greedy Might, the only force that works, which was conceived by primeval folk, born of emergent need, refined in aggressive climate, was modified, strengthened, polished: and defended like hell; and a Third Way arose in its tread; it fermented like leaven, and spreadeth throughout the land, that all should come to judge a bloke by his bread.

I believe in owning shares; the lowly plastic crutch; the extension of credit; the retention of gain; the reclamation of debt; and in life without fasting.

Amen

## The opposite of greed

Greed put in danger the social harmony of the early church, which was by and large made up of close-knit communities. We need only consider the marked social dimension of the moral teaching of the New Testament, with its frequent 'one another' teaching ('love one another', 'serve one another', 'bear one another's burdens', and so on), the description of the shared communal life of Christians in Acts and the use of kinship language throughout the New Testament (believers address each other as brother or sister).

In the second century, Christians became known not for their doctrinaire pronouncements or political astuteness, but rather for the way they shared their possessions with one another in the community.

Lucian of Samosata, a pagan travelling lecturer and rhetorician with no direct interest in Christianity, supplies remarkable confirmation of this assertion. He comments incredulously on the eager willingness of Christians to support their travelling delegates 'at their own expense ... for in no time they lavish their all'. His explanation stresses Christian belief in resurrection:

> The poor wretches have convinced themselves, first and foremost, that they are going to be immortal and live for all time ... Therefore they despise all things indiscriminately and consider them common property, receiving such doctrines traditionally without any

definite evidence. So if any charlatan and trickster, able to profit by occasions, comes among them, he quickly acquires sudden wealth by imposing upon simple folk.[1]

It is clear from Paul's speech to the Ephesian elders at Miletus that giving is the opposite of greed. At the end of the speech (Acts 20:32–35), Paul draws attention to the fact that during his ministry in Ephesus he worked at his trade so that he would not be a financial burden to the Ephesians ('I have not coveted anyone's silver or gold or clothing') and so that he might be in a position to support 'the weak' with money that he had earned. He cites 'the words the Lord Jesus himself said' to support the latter point. The saying is commonly translated (as in NIV) as comparing the states of the giver and the beneficiary: 'It is more blessed to give than to receive.' This sentiment, however, seems rather odd. Did Jesus really intend to cast aspersions on the blessing of receiving by comparing it unfavourably with that of giving? Most of us would affirm that as good as giving is, receiving is not that bad either.

The word 'to receive' can also mean 'to take hold of', and in this context this makes better sense. The 'receiving/taking' which is being unfavourably compared to 'giving' is not that of the needy who are being supported, 'the weak,' but rather of the ones who have worked and have the opportunity of sharing their possessions and pass up the opportunity. Paul is saying it was better for him to share his possessions than to keep them all to himself. The Jewish moral tractate Tobit (second century BC) makes a similar point: 'It is better to give alms than to treasure up gold' (12:8b). Acts 20:35b might be translated: 'It is more blessed to give than to keep.'

## The significance of giving

When we think of giving, it is usually in terms of money, and more specifically coins or notes dropped into an offertory plate or container. The main terms we use are 'charity' and 'donation'. The situation was quite different in the early church, where giving more often took in not just money but possessions generally, and was characterized more concretely as 'hospitality' and 'almsgiving'.

The New Testament notion of hospitality had nothing to do with impressing your friends at a dinner party in the hope of enjoying a nice meal in return. Rather, it consisted of *concrete, personal expressions of Christian love to fellow-believers*. It served as a positive practice to counter and expose greed.

Hospitality took a number of forms. It included meeting the pressing physical needs of the local poor, strangers and travelling Christians. The first missionaries travelled widely and were welcomed in a variety of homes (Acts 16:15, 32–34; 18:1–11), not just to make them feel at home, but to make it possible for them to carry on their ministry. Hospitality also included providing somewhere for believers to meet (Rom. 16:3–5, 23; Col. 4:15) when they came together for prayer, fellowship or to celebrate the Lord's Supper. It was a concrete way of expressing the respect and recognition called for in groups which were socio-economically and religiously diverse.

Hospitality, however, was not a mere practical expedient. After all, it didn't always work. Shared meals sometimes exposed tensions and inequalities in the church (Acts 10 – 11; 1 Cor. 11:17–34; Gal. 2:11–14; James 2:1–13). And it is not as if the church did not have other options. They could have gone for homogeneous churches (one for artisans, another for slaves, another for Jews, and so on). Or they could have abandoned the whole idea of the church as a community (which might have been difficult, since that is what the Greek word for 'church' means), and instead run a form of religious cinema, with people coming to enjoy the experience of worship or hear the preacher without bothering to relate to each other. The idea of bringing those of different classes and backgrounds together was just as alien then as it is now.

There was in fact a clear and irresistible theological warrant for hospitality. The notion of the incarnation with Jesus as a stranger on earth (cf. Luke 2:7; 4:16–30; 9:58; John 1:10–11), dependent on the generous support of others (cf. Luke 8:1–3; 9:1–6; 10:3–12, 38–42), made a permanent impression on early Christians. Not surprisingly, Matthew 25:21–46, Luke 14:12–14 and Hebrews 13:2 stress hospitality to strangers. The Greek word for 'hospitality' (cf. Rom. 12:13; Heb. 13:2; 1 Pet. 4:9;

1 Tim. 3:2; Titus 1:8) literally means 'love for the stranger'. Further, in the Gospels the presence of the kingdom is revealed in shared meals, such as in Luke 24:13–35, where Jesus turns the tables and appears not as guest but as host, and the disciples recognize him as their risen Lord. Paul urged believers to 'Welcome one another', as Christ had welcomed them (Rom. 15:7, Revised Standard Version).

The related responsibility, to show mercy in almsgiving (the Greek term for which is connected to the word for 'mercy') likewise had a profound theological basis. Such acts of compassion were to distinguish Christians as living advertisements of God's mercy in Christ. As those who have freely received, believers are freely to give. Charitable giving as the proper response to God's mercy was considered a mark of true spirituality. The ancient Jews taught that 'almsgiving endures for ever' (Sirach 40:17b) and that God takes particular notice of our charitable deeds: 'A man's almsgiving is like a signet with the Lord, and he will keep a person's kindness like the apple of his eye' (Sirach 17:22).

In Luke 11:41, almsgiving is valued more highly than matters of ritual purity, and in Luke 12:33 it is a mark of true discipleship. Such acts of mercy were highly regarded in the early church (Acts 9:36; 10:2) and were taken to be the regular obligation of Christians (cf. Acts 24:17). Generosity is a fruit of the Spirit (in the New Revised Standard Version of Gal. 5:22; usually translated 'kindness'), and liberal giving is a gift of the Spirit (Rom. 12:8). On the day of judgment, one thing the Son of Man will want to know is whether we have (unself-consciously) carried out acts of mercy on behalf of those in need (Matt. 25:31–46).

'It's enough for a man to understand his own business, and not to interfere with other people's. Mine occupies me constantly.'[2] So growled Ebenezer Scrooge in Charles Dickens' *A Christmas Carol*, until, that is, he had been pardoned by 'the Spirits'. Following this life-changing experience, Scrooge gave up his odious, stingy, cold, unfeeling, tight-fisted, closed-hearted ways. Christians ought to be able to identify with Scrooge's transformation.

One example of a Victorian businessman who would have made an excellent role model for the new Scrooge (a name change might also have helped) is the founder of Hartley's the jam-makers, Sir William Hartley (1846–1922). Hartley rose from humble origins to build a highly successful business which is still going today. He was known in his own day, however, far more for his amazing career of Christian philanthropy than for his impressive business acumen. At the age of twenty-nine he vowed to follow a course of systematic and proportionate giving, which held that as one's income grows, so should the percentage of money set aside for giving. In Hartley's opinion, 'nothing raises money to a higher plane and gives it a higher interest than systematic giving. I sit on my money; I don't let it sit on me. To distribute my money is a harder and more anxious task than making it.'[3]

Hartley did not find his commitment to giving easy, and he spoke often of the obstinacy of the selfish nature which we all share. His experience was that, in his own words, 'the adoption of an enlightened policy is generally a gradual process, but the more we cultivate the spirit of Jesus Christ, the easier the thing becomes; and what appeared to us quite impossible at the beginning becomes not only possible but absolutely a joy'.[4] Unlike the old Scrooge, Hartley regularly and voluntarily increased wages, practised profit-sharing and supplied low-cost, high-quality housing to some of his employees and free medical attention to all of them. He was also concerned for his suppliers, and would amend contracts in their favour if a change in the price of fruit and economic circumstances conspired against their making a decent living.

## Taking up the collection

It normally takes just a minute or two in a church service for the obligatory offering. It might be collected during a hymn or it might be accompanied by awkward or embarrassed silence. Either way, to any outsider present it seems at best routine and at worst peripheral, or even irrelevant, to the worship. By contrast, Paul once took up a collection for the poor saints in Jerusalem that occupied much of his time and energy for more than five years (from the early 50s).

For whatever reason (perhaps a prolonged famine) the churches in Jerusalem were poor and badly in need of relief. Paul took for granted the solidarity of believers in Christ and called on the goodwill of the many churches in the east of the Roman Empire. It appears that this campaign for funds was a major focus of his second missionary journey. The gift was to symbolize the unity of both Jews and Gentiles in Christ (Rom. 15:27). He regarded it as an act of fellowship (Rom. 15:27, 'shared') and compares it to a sacrificial offering (Rom. 15:31, 'my service in Jerusalem'; 2 Cor. 8:20; 9:1, 12–13), an act of worship in and of itself. Whereas for us a cup of tea or coffee might symbolize Christian fellowship, Paul's idea of fellowship brought to mind a wallet or a cheque-book.

He treats the matter of the collection at length in 2 Corinthians 8 – 9, where the Corinthians are encouraged to finalize their contribution to the campaign. A number of principles for giving emerge from his appeal. Christians ought to share their possessions generously (8:2; 9:6, 13), enthusiastically (8:4, 11–12; 9:7), deliberately (9:7) and sensibly (8:11–15). They are to follow the supreme example of Christ, who gave up the wealth of his heavenly existence, becoming (materially) 'poor' for the benefit of others, namely us, so that we might become (spiritually) 'rich' (8:8–9). Paul also appeals to the example of the churches of Macedonia (8:1–5, 8), suggesting that as the world competes in getting rich, Christians ought to invert such aims and compete in being generous. And he endorses the principle of reciprocity, whereby fellow-believers supply each other's needs from their abundance, expecting nothing less in return should the situation some day be reversed (8:14).

Much of this seems to run up against the whole notion of privacy and confidentiality in giving. Didn't Jesus say, 'when you give to the needy, do not let your left hand know what your right hand is doing' (Matt. 6:3)? What business was it of the Corinthians to know that the Macedonians had given so handsomely? How can one Christian reciprocate the generosity of another unless both parties are in the know? And since a main form of giving was hospitality, wouldn't everyone notice which hands were serving the meals, hosting the meetings and supplying the lodgings?

It appears that we may have taken Jesus' instructions to an extreme and, in the process, diminished the essential collegiality and accountability of Christian giving. Many have turned Jesus' call to pure motives into an excuse to expect others to mind their own business. Jesus was concerned to combat that natural human tendency to ostentation and play-acting; he opposed the giving which is done in order to make ourselves look good in the eyes of others, which remains a real and powerful temptation. He did not, however, intend to drive the practice of giving underground, as is clear from the following verses, in which he counsels that to avoid the hypocrisy of praying to impress others we ought to pray alone in secret (Matt. 6:5–6). Just as he had no intention of opposing all forms of corporate or group prayer, so also he did not wish to undercut the inevitable social dimension of giving and its essentially open and personal character.

# The profile of an average Christian

In religion, as in sport and politics, groups define themselves not just by saying what they stand for and who they are, but also in terms of what they oppose and who they aren't. One group of supporters will insist not only that their team is known for its enterprising, attacking play, but also that their main rivals take a stifling, negative, defensive approach to the game. Political parties often stake their claim to being economically responsible or socially just by accusing the other parties of not living up to these ideals. The early Christians, as we pointed out in chapter 1, had no trouble in describing those who were outside their group: your average pagan worshipped idols, was sexually immoral and greedy. This was not so much a sober description of every individual who did not acknowledge Christ as Lord, as a way of asserting the core values of their own group.

If a local church today were asked to draw up a profile of your average Christian, I wonder what it would look like. It might refer to matters of piety like Bible reading, prayer and church attendance. When Aristides, the converted Athenian Greek philosopher, attempted to characterize the Christians around AD 150, it was to the positive counterparts to idolatry, sexual immorality and greed that he pointed. First, Christians are those who 'worship no other God than him ... God the Creator and Maker of all things ... They do not worship strange gods.' Furthermore, 'their wives ... are pure as virgins and their daughters modest, and their men refrain from all unlawful intercourse and all uncleanness'. And finally, 'if they see a stranger, they bring him under their roof ... if they hear that any of their number is imprisoned or oppressed ... all of them provide for his needs ... And if there is among them a man that is poor and needy ... they fast two or three days that they may supply the needy with the necessary food.'

In the early church, the sharing of possessions was thus just as central to what it means to be a Christian as are the exclusive worship of the true God and the matter of sexual purity. Christians in the first or second century would have been just as perplexed to find a confessing Christian who worshipped idols or was openly adulterous as they would have been to meet one who refused to share his or her possessions. Paul thought giving so basic that he enjoined the former thief to 'work, doing something useful with his own hands [not so that he can look after himself, but so] that he may have something to share with those in need' (Eph. 4:28). Whereas our first concern for those out of work is that they may find a job in order to become self-supporting, Paul's was that they might be in a position to support others.

Rather than seeing themselves as individuals who happened to be Christians, the earliest Christians regarded themselves in the first place as members of the body of Christ, and took for granted their obligations to support one another, materially when necessary. Whatever might be said about the appropriate channels and methods of giving today, it should not escape our notice how far we have drifted from this point of view. A rich Christian may not be a contradiction in terms, but a mean and greedy Christian certainly is.

# 8
# TRUE RICHES

There are many different sorts of rivalries in the various realms of human endeavour. Some engender mutual respect. This is true in many cases of sporting competition, whether the activity be athletics, chess, boxing or ice-skating. There have of course been famous exceptions where the opponents experienced little love for each other, and sometimes may even have wished their opponents ill (in ice-skating, Tonya Harding for Nancy Kerrigan, for instance; and in boxing, Mike Tyson for Evander Holyfield). Such animosity is more often the case in politics, and occurs almost without exception where two men are competing for the affections of the same woman. In such circumstances a better word to describe what the rivals feel for each other is 'contempt' rather than respect. And each is perhaps keener than ever to assert not just his own better qualities but his superiority to the other man on offer.

Oddly enough, as we saw in chapter 2, when God competes with money for our affection it is sometimes to amorous human relationships that he compares the rivalry. He experiences jealousy whenever human beings turn their back on him to worship idols. Riches threaten to replace God in the same way that the 'other man' is a threat to a marriage. Accordingly, in order to keep his bride, God not only runs down the opposition (stressing the futility and transience of riches) but also offers more than his rival. In other words, at the risk of sounding crass, if Mammon offers to make us rich, God promises to outbid him. The difference is that God's protestations of superiority over the other suitor, as so rarely in the human realm, are neither doubtful nor debatable. The riches God offers are in reality of far greater worth.

## Better than gold

Just about everybody would like to get really rich. This is something that God realizes and uses to his advantage.

One of the substances most frequently mentioned in the Bible is gold. The supreme value, permanence and durability of gold are in no way disputed. Gold is associated with riches and power (Is. 60:17), characterized King Solomon's greatness (he 'made silver and gold as common in Jerusalem as stones'; 2 Chr. 1:15), and was one of the three gifts presented to the infant Jesus by the wise men (Matt. 2:11).

The marvel is that God offers something of even more value than gold. God's laws are more precious than gold (Ps. 19:10). Wisdom from God is a better investment than gold (Prov. 3:14, wisdom 'yields better returns than gold'; 8:10; 16:16). In fact, heaven itself is a city of pure gold (Rev. 21:18, 21). Most importantly, in place of an excessive attachment to material wealth, God himself is to be our gold: 'assign your nuggets to the dust, your gold of Ophir to the rocks in the ravines, then the Almighty will be your gold' (Job 22:24–25).

If the attraction of wealth is the prospect of enjoying an abundance of material goods, it is no accident that the Bible uses the language of abundance for spiritual goodness: God's abundant goodness (Pss. 31:19; 145:7), mercy (Pss. 51:1; 69:16), power (Ps. 145:7), grace (Rom. 5:17), salvation, wisdom and knowledge (Is. 33:6) bring to his people consolation (2 Cor. 1:5), joy (2 Cor. 8:2) and peace (2 Pet. 1:2) in abundance.

The promise of true riches both now and in the age to come is also offered in the New Testament, and frequently in the context of, and as a comfort in, financial loss. There are many examples.

In Mark 10:29–30, Jesus promises that those who have left homes or fields for his sake will receive a hundred times as much in return to make up for their losses.

In 1 Corinthians 6:9–11, Paul encourages Christians to suffer being defrauded (6:7–8) with the promise of inheriting God's kingdom.

In 2 Corinthians 8:9, Paul reminds the Corinthians of their becoming rich through Christ's poverty in part to undergird his plea for their involvement in the collection for the poor in Jerusalem.

In Philippians 4:19, the Philippian Christians are promised blessing 'according to [God's] glorious riches in Christ Jesus' in return for their financial contribution to Paul's support.

1 Timothy 6:5–6 turns the tables on the false teachers (who are looking to get rich through religion) by asserting that godliness with contentment brings great spiritual (rather than material) gain.

The rich in 1 Timothy 6:18–19 are to be 'rich in good deeds' by giving generously, thereby laying up 'treasure for themselves as a firm foundation for the coming age'.

In Hebrews 10:34, those who 'joyfully accepted the confiscation of [their] property' did so in the knowledge that they have 'better and lasting possessions'.

Paul described himself paradoxically as 'having nothing, but possessing everything' (2 Cor. 6:10).

The most graphic example appears at the end of Revelation, where the people of God who are told to 'come out' of doomed Babylon with all her riches (18:4) are given a vision of the new Jerusalem which more than compensates. If Babylon's wealth is to fall, the new Jerusalem's wealth is eternal and incorruptible: 'It shone with the glory of God, and its brilliance was like that of a very precious jewel, like a jasper, clear as crystal' (21:11). The 'fine linen' which clothed the 'great city' in 18:16 is eclipsed by the 'fine linen' which adorns the Lamb's bride in 19:8. The new Jerusalem's wealth far outweighs that which Revelation's readers are called to shun.

Thus young people who give up a lucrative career and the prospect of financial security to pursue aid work or full-time Christian service often see the matter in an entirely different light from those who look on and admire (or deride) their willingness to forgo riches. From their own point of view they have done nothing of the sort. When they sing the fourth verse of 'Be Thou my vision, O Lord of my heart',[1] a hymn which derives from an eighth-century Irish poem, they mean it:

> Riches I heed not, nor man's empty praise,
> Thou mine inheritance now and always;
> Thou, and thou only, first in my heart,
> High King of heaven, my treasure thou art.

Believers whose faith has somehow cost them materially are not thinking straight if they reckon they have missed out. Echoing the sentiments of Jesus, who said you'd be better off passing up the whole world if it meant forfeiting your soul (Matt. 16:26), the missionary and martyr Jim Elliot once observed, 'He is no fool who gives what he cannot keep to gain what he cannot lose.' Similarly, the great nineteenth-century Baptist preacher Charles Haddon Spurgeon observed: 'We need not covet money, for we shall always have our God, and God is better than gold, his favour is better than fortune.'[2]

## Finding treasure

Perhaps the most disturbing text on wealth in the entire Bible is Revelation 3:17–18, where some who say, 'I am rich; I have acquired wealth and do not need a thing' (the unwritten slogan of many a well-to-do suburb) are described as 'wretched, pitiful, poor, blind and naked'. They are told to 'buy ... gold refined in the fire, so that you can become rich' in order to remedy the situation. But surely this advice is preposterous at best, and at worst cruel and perverse. How can those described as 'poor' ever hope to afford fine gold? You may as well tell a blind person to read print, or an infant to run a marathon. This is of course to read the verses in a naïvely literalistic fashion. The non-literal use of the notion of riches is well known. Outside of the religious sphere, people sometimes talk of having their lives *enriched* by grandchildren, music or a garden, none of which has anything to do with money. And social commentators have always distinguished between 'standard of living' (a purely economic measure) and 'quality of life'.

The figurative use of the notions of poverty and riches in Revelation 3 is clearly meant to signify two things. First, those who are materially rich may not be really rich. Secondly, and even more alarmingly, spiritual riches are by no means within their budget. It recalls Isaiah's engaging invitation to 'Come ... you who have no money ... Come, buy ... without money and without cost' (55:1).

The command to buy fine gold, like the surprising

description of the rich as actually being poor, is deliberately worded to give those who are smug and self-satisfied, those who think they are doing rather well thank you very much, pause for thought. Verses 19–20 give some indication as to what is meant, using the old-fashioned word 'repentance'. If we are rich and want to get really rich, we are to start by admitting our spiritual bankruptcy, turn from our proud self-sufficiency and accept Jesus' offer of a personal relationship and friendship ('Here I am! I stand at the door and knock', verse 20). In other words, we must seek God, in the firm knowledge that we will find him only because in the first place he is seeking us.

The Christian gospel of acceptance with God, not on the basis of what we do but on what he has done (in sending his Son to secure our release from the power and penalty of sin), uses a variety of expressions to instruct us how we ought to respond. The most familiar are faith (towards God) and repentance (from sin). The same action, however, can be characterized as receiving (Christ), obeying (his authoritative summons), hearing (his call), and, more metaphorically, as waking up (from a deep sleep), drinking (his Spirit), eating (Christ's flesh) and buying (his gold). They all mean basically the same thing. The last expression is particularly apt for those who consider themselves to be rich, for it simultaneously registers with them (they are used to such transactions) and horrifies them (they can't afford it).

If buying fine gold (in this letter to the church in

Laodicea) signifies the way of entry into a personal relationship with God, two other purchases (verse 18) indicate what will result from this act of repentance.

First, the Laodiceans' 'shameful nakedness' would be remedied by buying 'white clothes to wear'. Nakedness is a biblical symbol for humiliation on the day of judgment, fine clothes for honour and forgiveness. In Revelation, white clothes in particular are worn by those who live in the presence of God (cf. 3:4–5; 4:4; 7:9; 19:14). Revelation 7:14 explains that such robes have been washed in the blood of the Lamb. The harshness of the condemnation of the 'rich' in this passage is more than matched by the magnanimous offer of mercy and restoration. It is out of love that the rebuke is offered in the first place (3:19). Once we arrive at the point of admitting the folly of the sin of greed, there is available to us full pardon and complete forgiveness on the basis of Christ's sacrificial death. It is simply a matter of getting dressed.

One of the biggest obstacles for many people in relation to this much-misunderstood business of repentance towards God is that it all sounds too good to be true. Often the problem is not unbelief so much as disbelief. The truth is, however, that what so many of us crave is exactly what is on offer, namely a fresh start. When Zacchaeus, the greedy tax collector, came to Jesus (Luke 19:1–10), it was the crowd, not Jesus, who regarded him as literally beyond redemption. Jesus took the initiative and invited himself into Zacchaeus' house. Zacchaeus' decision to open the door led to Jesus' startling affirmation that 'Today salvation has come to this house' and to his own radical about-turn: 'Here and now I give half of my possessions to the poor, and if I have cheated anybody out of anything, I will pay back four times the amount.'

Secondly, the Laodiceans' 'blindness' would be remedied by buying 'salve' to put on their eyes, so they could see. As we noted in chapter 3, greed is basically a problem of vision. What you see is what you get, or at least what you try to get. Those who repent are promised not only forgiveness but also transformation, resulting from authentic healing. They have the opportunity to stop behaving like everyone else in town and act out a new set of priorities and values. In short, they will see things differently and act accordingly, or see something better than material things and go after it.

Strictly speaking, the Bible's solution to greed is not to stop wanting to be rich. To expect that of human beings would be unrealistic. There is no point just telling people to stop seeking and running after riches. Such desires need to be not quashed so much as redirected. In Colossians 3, believers are not only to put to death earthly greed, which is idolatry (3:5), but also and instead to set their minds on things above, not on earthly things (3:1–2). Likewise, in the context of Jesus' saying that you cannot serve God and Money/Mammon, the teaching against greed is introduced with the injunction to lay up treasures not on earth but in heaven (Matt. 6:19), and closes with the call to seek first God's kingdom and righteousness (verse 33) instead of the material things which the Gentiles seek (verse 32). In 1 Timothy 6:10–11 it is not enough just to run away from greed; the godly person is also to run after something: the way to flee the love of money is to pursue God and godly virtues.

The importance of replacing evil desires with holy ones was seen by the Church Father Augustine, who wrote, 'Let not these occupy my soul; rather let God occupy it.'[3] True riches consist of having a stake in the life of the true and living God. To recall the two texts upon which the reflections of this book have been based, if 'greed … is idolatry' (Col. 3:5), and you are disinclined to place too much stock on material things, then it is worth remembering that 'godliness with contentment is great gain' (1 Tim. 6:6).

If the greedy find pleasure and fulfilment in their possessions, in God's presence we are filled with joy and at his right hand are eternal pleasures (Ps. 16:11). The task and privilege of the Christian is to glorify God, but also to enjoy him. Human beings are incomplete and ultimately dissatisfied until they are right with God, who, at great cost – not that of silver and gold, but of the blood of his dear Son – has purchased our redemption. What we see around us is not all there is and ever will be. We can fight God, or ignore him, or replace him with any manner of substitutes, including material wealth; but to do any of these is futile and a folly and can only lead to disappointment.

If the greedy look to their riches for confidence

and security, God offers a far superior and harder currency, one which has no risk of exposure to instability or devaluation. The person who is really rich has come to a settled confidence and trust in God, who made the world and everything in it. Such a person affirms that 'There is no-one like ... God ... The eternal God is [my] refuge, and underneath are the everlasting arms' (Deut. 33:26–27). Even if an economic (or natural) disaster comes upon them, they affirm with Paul that nothing 'will be able to separate us from the love of God that is in Christ Jesus' (Rom. 8:35–39).

If the greedy eventually find themselves in a demeaning and destructive slavery to Mammon, resenting their bondage, the person who is really rich has discovered true liberty and freedom in serving God, who himself took the form of a servant in Christ. The train is truly free only when it runs on the tracks, and, however inviting the alternative might appear, it would come to a grinding halt if it were free to plough into the field. 'If the Son sets you free, you will be free indeed' (John 8:36).

## Having your cake

But does it have to be 'either/or'? Can't a person be both materially rich and rich towards God at the same time? Why not aim at both sorts of riches? The Bible doesn't, in fact, rule out the possibility; calls to voluntary poverty are fairly rare, and the rich are not always told to give it all away. But neither does the Bible encourage such thinking; it is never shy of questioning our motives and underscoring our proneness to self-deception. Seeking God is meant to be a life-long, all-consuming, all-embracing passion, which does not so much rule out the goal of getting rich as squeeze it out.

The Jewish philosopher Philo of Alexandria, who was a contemporary of Paul, asked with great insight, 'of what riches can we any longer stand in need, when we have you, who alone is true riches?'[4] In the final analysis it is a matter of priorities. Which do you crave more, to be rich, or to be really rich?

Desire not only orders our lives, it also informs our prayers. Proverbs 30:8–9 contains a prayer which strikes the right balance:

> Give me neither poverty nor riches,
>    but give me only my daily bread.
> Otherwise, I may have too much and disown
>       you
>    and say, 'Who is the Lord?'
> Or I may become poor and steal,
>    and so dishonour the name of my God.

The danger that wealth will lead to pride and blasphemy means that for most of us it is simply better not to get rich. The pitfalls of both poverty and wealth seem so inevitable that the prayer asks (literally) for 'food of my portion', no more and no less – a modest sufficiency. Wealth often leads to feeling we have no need of God and ultimately to denying him. It is better to be denied wealth than to have wealth and to deny God.

## An eight-step plan for getting really rich

The following points summarize the chapters of the book in turn:

1. **G**ag greed
2. **E**schew idolatry
3. **T**arget love

4. **A**void futility

5. **L**ove liberty
6. **I**ndulge contentment
7. **F**urnish aid
8. **E**xalt God

In chapter 4 we met those aboard the good ship *Cherished Wealth* on their 'voyage of conviction' (p. 71). The above acrostic recalls their parting shot, which was directed at those who refused to jump aboard. As put-downs go, 'Get a life' is steeply condescending and devastatingly comprehensive. It may be turned on its head, however, and said to those who mistakenly think that life is about material possessions, that life consists of food and the body of clothing (cf. Matt. 6:25b).

'Get a life' in fact summarizes the Bible's ultimate diagnosis of what's wrong with greed, and prescribes its most effective cure. Jesus summed up his mission in terms of bringing life in its abundance (John 10:10). Deuteronomy 30:19 calls us to 'choose life', not as a nasty taunt, but as a winsome invitation.

And 1 Timothy 6, which offers a warning against the love of money, concludes by exhorting its readers to 'take hold of the life that is truly life' (verse 19b).

> Godliness with contentment is great gain. For we brought nothing into the world, and we can take nothing out of it. But if we have food and clothing, we will be content with that. People who want to get rich fall into temptation and a trap and into many foolish and harmful desires that plunge men into ruin and destruction. For the love of money is a root of all kinds of evil. Some people, eager for money, have wandered from the faith and pierced themselves with many great griefs.
>
> But you, man of God, ought to flee from all this, and pursue righteousness, godliness, faith, love, endurance and gentleness. Fight the good fight of the faith. Take hold of the eternal life to which you were called ...
>
> Command those who are rich in this present world not to be arrogant nor to put their hope in wealth, which is so uncertain, but to put their hope in God, who richly provides us with everything for our enjoyment. Command them to do good, to be rich in good deeds, and to be generous and willing to share. In this way they will lay up treasure for themselves as a firm foundation for the coming age, so they may take hold of the life that is truly life.
>
> (1 Tim. 6:6–12a, 17–19)

# Notes

## Preface

1. For this, see Craig Blomberg, *Neither Poverty nor Riches: A Biblical Theology of Possessions* (Leicester: Apollos, 1999).

## 1. Unmasking greed

1. Dorothy Rowe, *The Real Meaning of Money* (London: HarperCollins, 1997), pp. 148–151.
2. Reported in Robert Wuthnow, *God and Mammon in America* (New York: The Free Press, 1994), p. 126.
3. Miroslav Volf, 'In the Cage of Vanities: Christian Faith and the Dynamics of Economic Progress', in Robert Wuthnow (ed.), *Rethinking Materialism: Perspectives on the Spiritual Dimension of Economic Behaviour* (Grand Rapids: Eerdmans, 1995), p. 172.
4. Albert Barnes, *Notes Explanatory and Practical on the*

*Epistles of Paul* (New York: Harper Brothers, 1845), p. 317.

5. George Harrison in *The Times*, 28 August 1995, p. 5.
6. Reported in Rowe, *The Real Meaning of Money*, p. 206.
7. *The Times Magazine*, 15 August 1998, p. 36.
8. *The Times*, 18 March 1998, p. 25.
9. *The Guardian*, 25 March 1996.
10. Philo, *On the Contemplative Life* 17.
11. 1QS 11:1–2.
12. *Mekilta* Exodus 20:17.
13. Zeno of Verona, *On Greed* 1.11.
14. Basil the Great, *Sermon to the Rich* 5.
15. Solomon Schimmel, *The Seven Deadly Sins* (New York: The Free Press, 1992), p. 18.
16. Rowe, *The Real Meaning of Money*, p. ix.
17. Rowe, *The Real Meaning of Money*, p.184.
18. Cited by Volf, 'In the Cage of Vanities', p. 172.
19. Jüngel, 'Gewinn in Himmel und auf Erden: Theologische Bemerkungen zum Streben und Gewinn', *Zeitschrift für Theologie und Kirche* 94.4 (1997), p. 547.

## 2. Secret idolatry

1. E.g. Mishnah *Sanhedrin* 7:4, 6–7, 10; 11:1, 6.
2. David W. Bercot, *A Dictionary of Early Christian Beliefs* (Peabody, MA: Hendrickson, 1998), p. 350.
3. Whether worship of the belly in Rom. 16:18 and Phil. 3:19 refers to Jewish preoccupation with food laws or circumcision, fleshly egocentricism or gluttony and (by extension) greed, is difficult to say.
4. John Boli, 'The Economic Absorption of the Sacred', in Robert Wuthnow (ed.), *Rethinking Materialism: Perspectives on the Spiritual Dimension of Economic Behaviour* (Grand Rapids: Eerdmans, 1995), p. 95. My analysis of the religion of money builds upon that of Boli and Miroslav Volf (in the same volume).
5. Dorothy Rowe, *The Real Meaning of Money* (London:

HarperCollins, 1997), p. 54.

6.  Boli, 'The Economic Absorption of the Sacred', p. 113.
7.  Alan Storkey, 'Postmodernism and Consumption', in *Christ and Consumption*, edited by Craig Bartholomew and Thorsten Moritz (Carlisle: Paternoster, forthcoming).

## 3. Inordinate love

1.  Edited by Lesley Brown. Vol. 2: N–Z, p. 3723.
2.  cf. *Oxford English Dictionary* (2nd edition, 1989), definition of an idol: 'Any thing or person that is the object of excessive or supreme *devotion* or that usurps the place of God in human *affection*' (vol. 7, p. 29, my italics). *Collins English Dictionary and Thesaurus* (Glasgow: HarperCollins, 1993), p. 1348, defines worship in similar terms as 'admiring love or devotion'.
3.  Homily II.20 (*Patrologia Latina* 155, p. 2013), my italics.
4.  John Calvin, *Sermons on the Epistle to the Ephesians* (Edinburgh: Banner of Truth, 1973), pp. 503–504, my italics.
5.  J. B. Lightfoot, *Epistle to the Colossians* (London: Macmillan, 1904), p. 210, my italics.
6.  *The Complete Works of George Orwell* 4: *Keep the Aspidistra Flying* (London: Secker and Warburg, 1987), p. 267.
7.  Augustine, *The City of God* 11.25.
8.  Augustine, *On Various Questions* 83.30.
9.  Justo L. González, *Faith and Wealth: A History of Early Christian Ideas on the Origin, Significance, and Use of Money* (San Francisco: Harper and Row, 1990), p. 216.
10. Clarkson, *Works* 2 (Edinburgh: Banner of Truth, 1988), p. 300.
11. Clarkson, *Works* 2, p. 300.
12. Clarkson, *Works* 2, p. 301.
13. Clarkson, *Works* 2, p. 307.

14. Clarkson, *Works* 2, p. 302: 'Love, whenever it is inordinate, is an idolatrous affection.'
15. Clarkson, *Works* 2, pp. 305–306.
16. Clarkson, *Works* 2, p. 306.
17. Clarkson, *Works* 2, p. 313.
18. D. M. Lloyd-Jones, *Darkness and Light: An Exposition of Ephesians 4:17 – 5:17* (Edinburgh: Banner of Truth, 1982), p. 340.
19. Cf. the same targums to Prov. 3:9, which have 'Honour the Lord with your mammon.'

## 4. Misplaced trust

1. *Daily Record*, 16 February 1999, p. 19.

## 5. Forbidden service

1. Cyprian, *Epistle* 1.12, my italics.
2. Cited in Solomon Schimmel, *The Seven Deadly Sins* (New York: The Free Press, 1992), p. 165.
3. Jacques Ellul, *Money and Power* (Southampton: Marshall Pickering, 1979), p. 76.
4. Charles Dickens, *A Christmas Carol* (Oxford: OUP, 1988), pp. 38–39.
5. Chrysostom, *Homilies on Galatians, Ephesians, Philippians, Colossians, Thessalonians, Timothy, Titus and Philemon* (Grand Rapids: Eerdmans, 1979). See especially the 18th homily on Ephesians.
6. Reported in Dorothy Rowe, *The Real Meaning of Money* (London: HarperCollins, 1997), p. 148.
7. Much of the following discussion builds on chapter 8 of Cornelius Plantinga, *Not the Way It's Supposed to Be: A Breviary of Sin* (Leicester: Apollos, 1995).
8. Karl Marx, *Writings of the Young Marx on Philosophy and Society* (New York: Doubleday, 1967), pp. 245–246. Moshe Halbertal and Avishai Margarlit, *Idolatry* (Cambridge: Harvard University Press, 1992), p. 43,

explain Marx's view further: 'The more man works the more he accumulates money, and the more he externalizes his essence to the alien god of money.' See also Stanford M. Lyman, *The Seven Deadly Sins: Society and Evil* (New York: General Hall, 1989), pp. 253–259, on Marx's characterization of money as 'omnipotent ... like a god' (p. 254).

9. Marx, *Writings of the Young Marx on Philosophy and Society*, pp. 289–290.

# 6. Learning contentment

1. Jeremiah Burroughs, *The Rare Jewell of Christian Contentment* (1648; Edinburgh: Banner of Truth, 1964), p. 46.
2. Burroughs, *The Rare Jewell*, p. 46.
3. Miroslav Volf, 'In the Cage of Vanities: Christian Faith and the Dynamics of Economic Progress', in Robert Wuthnow (ed.), *Rethinking Materialism: Perspectives on the Spiritual Dimension of Economic Behaviour* (Grand Rapids: Eerdmans, 1995), p. 171.
4. Cf. David T. Williams, 'Against the Tide: Christian Self-limitation', *EQ* 70.3 (1998), pp. 248–249.
5. Burroughs, *The Rare Jewell*, p. 83.
6. Burroughs, *The Rare Jewell*, p. 84.
7. Burroughs, *The Rare Jewell*, pp. 65, 67.
8. *Aboth* 4:1.
9. Thomas Manton, *The Complete Works* (Worthington, PA: Maranatha, n.d.), 2, p. 313.
10. Karl Barth, *Church Dogmatics* (Edinburgh: T. and T. Clark, 1958), 3.1, pp. 181ff.
11. See Susan L. Buckley, *Usury Friendly: The Ethics of Moneylending – A Biblical Interpretation* (Cambridge: Grove Books, 1998).
12. Cited in Timothy Gorringe, *Capital and the Kingdom: Theological Ethics and the Economic Order* (London: SPCK, 1994), p. 139.

13. See Paul Mills, *Interest in Interest: The Old Testament Ban on Interest and its Implications for Today* (Cambridge: Jubilee Centre Publications, 1993).
14. Burroughs, *The Rare Jewell*, p. 33.
15. Quoted in Wuthnow (ed.), *Rethinking Materialism*, p. 179.
16. Burroughs, *The Rare Jewell*, p. 21.
17. Burroughs, *The Rare Jewell*, p. 43.

## 7. Sharing possessions

1. *On the Death of Peregrinus* 1.
2. Charles Dickens, *A Christmas Carol* (1843; Oxford: OUP, 1988), p. 12.
3. Arthur S. Peake, *The Life of Sir William Hartley* (London: Hodder and Stoughton, 1926), p. 76.
4. Peake, *The Life of Sir William Hartley*, p. 78.
5. Aristides, *Apology* 15.1–10.

## 8. True riches

1. This hymn was translated from the original Gaelic into English in 1905 by Mary Byrne (1880–1931) and later versified by Eleanor Hull (1860–1935).
2. Cited in John Blanchard (ed.), *More Gathered Gold: A Treasury of Quotations for Christians* (Welwyn: Evangelical Press, 1986), p. 64.
3. Augustine, *Confessions* 10.51.
4. Philo, *On Dreams* 1.179.
5. Reported in *Third Way* 21.10 (December 1998), p. 5.